From SRN to CBE
Celebrating 50 remarkable years in nursing

From SRN to CBE
Celebrating 50 remarkable years
in nursing

by

Mary Spinks (formerly Donn)

QUAY
BOOKS

A division of MA Healthcare Ltd

Quay Books Division, MA Healthcare Ltd, St Jude's Church, Dulwich Road, London
SE24 0PB

British Library Cataloguing-in-Publication Data
A catalogue record is available for this book

ISBN-10: 1 85642 507 X
ISBN-13: 978 1 85642 507 0

Printed by Mongo Print, Bournemouth

Contents

Dedication

In loving memory of Leslie and dedicated to the inspirational nurses I met along the way.

Acknowledgements

My grateful thanks go to my dear friends, Pamela Mummery and Dr Anita White, who inspired me to write this book. I have been helped by my many friends and ex-colleagues, David Bowden, Gillian DeMarco, Roger Evans, Sheila Forde, Ray Greenwood, Janet King, Una Lynch, Lindy Maxwell, Stephanie Oates, Jane Reid, Liz Robb, Martin Smits, Geoffrey Walker, Mary-Lyn van der Watt and Brian Wilson.

My friends at the Association of Operating Room Nurses, especially MaryJo Steiert and her colleagues who updated me on the "USA scene".

To Mark Allen, Rebecca Linssen and Liz Rhodes of MA Healthcare who helped to bring the book to fruition.

My apologies to anyone that I have missed out.

FOREWORD

by Baroness Emerton, DBE, DL

What was it like 58 years ago to be released from a tight-knit family and the confines of a cloistered life in Ireland to cosmopolitan life in London and the regime of an East London nurse training school?

In this book author Mary Spinks (formerly Donn) describes how she adapted to the change in culture and settled into a programme of nurse training as it was ten years after the introduction of the NHS. Little did she think that this was in fact the beginning of a very successful career, ultimately recognised by the award of the Commander of the British Empire for her services to nursing.

I first met Mary in 1968, during the implementation of the Salmon Report. Her potential was already evident and proved by rapid promotion until she achieved the post of Regional Nursing Officer. Mary took an active interest in the development of nurse education as it moved away from local training schools into further education.

Mary's final position gave her the opportunity to pursue her passion for promoting and enabling scholarships for nurses intent on carrying out research to enhance quality care for patients. She became Director of the Florence Nightingale Foundation, which was dependent on charitable funding, and vigorously promoted a range of scholarships.

Mary has captured in this book the immense privilege of being a nurse.

Audrey Emerton

by Dr Peter Carter OBE

This text captures the evolution of nursing from the 1950s into the 21st century.

This is a beautifully written book in which Mary Spinks shares with the reader significant amount of personal disclosure concerning family relations, religious tensions and the undoubted love of her late husband Leslie.

It also captures the spirit of nursing over several decades and will be a lasting chronology for those researching the history and development of nursing not only in the UK but internationally.

It is also a testimonial to Mary's tenacity, intellect and her ability to embark on new ventures.

I feel privileged to be asked to write the foreword for this book and I hope it finds its place in the libraries of all nursing schools. I believe it will also be of interest to the broader public.

It represents a lifetime of commitment, achievement and will inspire the next and future generations of nurses.

Dr Peter Carter OBE
Chief Executive
Royal College of Nursing

Will this boat ever leave? That was what I was thinking as I stood on deck, tears streaming down my face. On the quayside stood my family, waving tear-stained handkerchiefs. I should have felt a sense of adventure at the prospect of starting a new life training to be a nurse; instead, all I felt was a great sadness and sense of loss.

We were a closely-knit family. There was not much money in the Ireland of the forties and fifties, but much loving and caring. This was intertwined with respect for our parents and elders, a degree of discipline and emphasis on educational achievement. Our teachers, both the nuns and the lay teachers, knew our family and had no doubt provided references to the matron at Whipps Cross Hospital where I was heading.

Whipps Cross Hospital was known as a bastion of Irish Catholicism. It had an Irish matron and a Catholic Church five minutes' walk away. Convent schools in Ireland had links with such institutions and many of us would not have been allowed to leave the country without such arrangements being in place. It is said that when the British pulled out of Ireland after it became a Republic in 1922, the Catholic Church took over as the powerful ruling body. This shows the influence of the Church on the Irish people and may, in some way, explain how some of the clergy maintained the abuse of the vulnerable over many years.

When Winston Churchill was canvassing near Whipps Cross in his constituency of Woodford Green one Sunday, some Irish nurses were heckling him and demanding that he give the six counties of Northern Ireland back to the Republic of Ireland. Churchill glared at them and declared 'I will give you back the six counties when you give us back Whipps Cross'.

Entrants to nursing in the teaching hospitals from Catholics in the Republic of Ireland were, on the whole, not welcome unless their families already had an involvement in medicine or nursing. Maybe it was for the same reason that, during the Crimean War, Florence Nightingale was allegedly concerned that the Sisters of Mercy in the Crimea would try to convert the soldiers to Catholicism.

I was born in 1940, the third of five children, with two older sisters, a younger sister and a brother, the youngest. My very happy childhood consisted of school and during holidays we helped out on my mother's family farm. Potato picking and harvesting the crops were busy times. Riding the horses, two Clydesdales, up to the upper fields for grazing during the night, was one of my highlights on summer evenings.

My father, who had spent his apprenticeship in the hardware business, owned and run by British firms, finally realised his great dream and opened his own business in 1949. At that time, the banks in Ireland, mainly still owned by the British, considered new businesses a high risk and my father was, therefore, refused a loan. Some friends and relatives lent him money and became shareholders until he could buy them out.

To his death, he always remembered that fact and never wanted to be indebted to banks. One can only wonder what he would have made of the banking situation today.

As the first Catholic hardware merchant in Cork, he was very popular with the nuns and priests in the many convents and monasteries that existed at that time. The nuns unfailingly provided a delicious tea for him, when he made his deliveries to the convents where he was always welcomed. The fare was not so appetising at Mound Melleray Abbey, where the monks led a frugal existence. I loved to accompany him on the trips to the convents, as it meant lots of cakes.

Although it was mainly 'ups' over the years, there were some 'downs'. One of the 'downs' was caused by the polio outbreak in 1956. Every business needs time to get established and the polio outbreak resulted in Cork city becoming a ghost city. The cause of the outbreak was never really established, so people shied away from contacts with others in crowded places.

It was at about this time that my thoughts turned to the future. Nursing in Ireland was almost the same as entering the convent, so that was out. My mother advised me that the family hardware business, already at risk because of the polio epidemic, would not support all of us children. Money was tight, university fees were expensive and it became clear that I should look further afield. Unemployment was high and the only professions open to girls were teaching and nursing. There was little sense of vocation and like so many Irish girls who came to nurse training in the fifties, I was an economic emigrant. The National Health Service, just ten years old in 1958, was expanding and more labour was needed. We were cheap labour. We were paid a pittance, but our board and food were all supplied free at that time.

So the plan was that I should go to Whipps Cross for the three years' training and then return to Cork to do my midwifery. As the plans progressed,

I felt I was in for an experience and an adventure. I did not realise what a big step it would be to leave a closely-knit family and I was to suffer from homesickness for many years.

Even as a child, I had been a show-off, an attention-seeker and an extrovert. I remember going dancing one evening, against my parents' wishes, while my elder sisters dutifully went to bed. This involved sneaking out through my bedroom window and getting back in the same way, but it was good practice for life at Whipps Cross.

WHIPPS CROSS

So here I was in November 1958, on the night boat from Cork to Fishguard, without any real idea of what lay ahead. I took the train from Fishguard to Paddington where I was met by my uncle. He took me to the Wilfred Lawson School in Woodford Green, where I was to spend the first three months of my training. It was called Preliminary Training School, where we learned to make beds, take each other's temperatures and blood pressure, and apply bandages. We needed to know how to clean everything we would encounter on the wards, including the furniture and floors. This was obviously to impress on us the importance of hygiene when nursing sick people. Unfortunately, with the introduction of antibiotics, this activity became of lesser importance with disastrous results, such as MRSA and other infections.

The Christmas of 1958 at Whipps Cross was one of the saddest and loneliest of my life. We had not really made friends and were sent to Whipps Cross for the two weeks over Christmas and New Year, to help out on the wards. We did not know the staff or patients and came back to the Wilfred Lawson each evening to watch television, something that had not yet arrived in Ireland. The television covered up the sniffles and silent crying, as many of us were thinking of family and what would be happening at home. We were all utterly homesick.

The entrants to the school of November 1958 were made up of approximately forty trainees, most of whom were Irish. There were two English girls, two girls from British Guiana (now Guyana) and two men from Nigeria. Of this assortment, the most fascinating were the two from Nigeria – Mr Danjuma and Mr Bui. Few of the Irish girls had ever met Africans before and did not know how to handle them. We learned that Mr Danjuma was the son of a chief of a tribe and expected us to open doors for him. We took great delight in slamming them in his face, something our parents would not have condoned. Political correctness was not even on the horizon. Notices such as 'No Blacks, No Irish, No dogs' had only recently been removed from boarding house windows.

The other Nigerian was, by contrast, a gentleman and often went to London in his time off wearing a trilby and carrying an umbrella. They did not live in the nurses' home as no men were allowed in at any time.

Student nurse training in my day was totally different from today. It was an apprentice type of training. We learned from the sisters and staff nurses on the wards and in the departments. We had periods of studying that were called 'block' and usually occurred before examinations. For our intake, Part I of the Preliminary State Examination was held in June 1959, Part II in February 1960 and we sat our Finals in February 1962.

Block consisted of two weeks in the classroom learning various procedures and techniques as well as having lectures. One procedure was setting up dressing trolleys and carrying out sterile wound dressings. This involved the use of Cheatle forceps for picking up everything from cotton wool balls to the dressings. These forceps were like large scissors without blades and were incredibly fiddly to use. Sterile rubber gloves took over from the forceps eventually.

We stood around the trolley while the sister tutor explained how the procedure was carried out. We took great delight in putting pieces of cotton wool on top of our Nigerian colleagues' frizzy hair. They never felt a thing, while the rest of the class had difficulty in controlling giggles.

We worked hard on the wards all day and studied during our breaks and in the evening. There were exams to pass and if we failed, we could be sent home. This would have meant returning to Ireland in disgrace, but at the same time, to go back to our families was what many of us craved.

That was a dilemma and when I underwent a medical, I thought I had found the solution; the occupational health doctor saw us all before we started on the wards. To my surprise and delight, I was referred to a cardiologist but was not informed why. I immediately thought that I might be able to go home due to ill health and that would not be a disgrace. It turned out that I only had a slow pulse because I had had an active childhood and because I was a keen swimmer and played tennis.

Night duty was a nightmare, especially in the summer. Our body clocks were out of rhythm and we were always tired. We had a tea break at about three in the morning and if the wards were quiet, we would spend the break wrapped in our cloaks, sleeping on a shelf in the linen cupboard. When we were woken by our colleagues, we felt even worse. We lost weight, as for some extraordinary reason we had breakfast in the evening before the night shift and then faced supper in the morning. I can see the red jelly and pink blancmange on the serving counter, when after a difficult night this was the last thing we wanted. There were small kitchens on each floor of the nurses' home, complete with a grill. We were supplied with bread and butter, so we lived on buttered toast and marmalade nicked from the ward kitchen.

On many wards, two students were the total staffing and a night sister would do rounds when drugs were needed. So in the good old days there were aspects that were not so good. This, of course, needs to be balanced against the types of illnesses and how patients were treated. Hospital stays were much longer compared to today; a hernia repair might result in a ten-day inpatient stay. A cataract extraction required complete bed rest for six weeks, with both eyes bandaged. This now requires a hospital stay of a few hours. There was no pressure on beds and patients would remain in hospital until the next lot of patients needed to be admitted. Most consultants had their own ward, with a ward sister who waited on them hand and foot. However the consultant had great respect for his ward sister and would seek her advice on the care of the patient. Pain was not as well controlled as it is today and I remember post-operative patients suffering great pain. Looking back there must have been a fear of addiction.

The matron, Miss Fogarty, would visit the wards, unannounced, to check on everything. She was not really unannounced as her dog, a corgi, was always ahead of her and would warn us that she was on the prowl. The next ward would be alerted by telephone and if we were sneaking a cup of tea in the sluice, the cups would get a temporary home in the linen bin.

The release from the tedium of studying was to get up to all sorts of escapades in the nurses' home at night after studying – no one was allowed to live outside for the first two years. One of the pranks organised by my close colleagues one night involved the laundry lift. This lift was small and was used to move laundry boxes to the various floors in the nurses' home. One night after hours of studying I was challenged to see if I could fit in the lift. This I managed, knees to chest, showing off as usual. Unaware that my colleagues had gone to other floors, I found myself going up and down between floors. I landed on the ground floor to find the assistant matron, who lived in the home, outside the lift, hair in curlers and furious at the noise. 'Get out!' was the order. I climbed down, dressed in my pink shorty pyjamas, and was humiliatingly marched back to my room. 'See me in my office in the morning' resulted in my being deprived of late passes for a period of time.

This was not really a deterrent as we came through the windows of the nurses' home more often than the door. The rule was that if you slept in a room on the ground floor, you had to have your bed under the window for easy access. Although we worked hard, we also played hard. It was no bother to us to come off duty, get dolled up and go off to London to an Irish club. We would get back to Leytonstone just before midnight. Whipps Cross was a long walk away so we used a department store's large doorway to hide in, while one of us stood on the pavement thumbing a lift. Some poor chap would pull up, thinking he had it made for the night and the rest of us would pile into the car. Sometimes a police car might pick us up and with siren wailing, we would speed through the gates at a minute to midnight when our late passes finished.

We found ourselves released from parental control, there was no closely-knit community where any misdemeanours would be fed back to our parents, and so we were running wild. The escapades were never shared with our families in the letters; they would have been appalled at such behaviour. At that time telephone calls to Ireland had to be booked. Three minutes cost three shillings and sixpence from the public telephone box in the nurses' home, a lot of money to a student nurse, but it was great to hear familiar voices although I spent most of my time crying such was my homesickness.

Most of our patients in the area of Whipps Cross were East Enders, the salt of the earth. Some were aware of how homesick we were and on discharge one of the patients invited us on a coach tour of the orchards in Kent, with a pub lunch thrown in. It was a beautiful day and many of the large number of fruit trees were in full bloom. One thing that surprised me when I first came to London was the amount of huge green spaces in the various parks. At home in Ireland, my impression was that London was nothing but streets of houses and shops, and the parks were an unexpected bonus.

It was inevitable that some of us would meet our future husbands as we went to more and more parties and unfortunately that happened to me. I met Bob at a wild party in London. He was Scottish, a journalist and an atheist, probably the worst combination for me to encounter. I was physically attracted to him and was convinced that I was in love. He was very flattering and I lapped it up. No one had paid me such attention before. He was still living in Scotland at the time, wrote me long letters and came to London for weekends. We spent Christmas 1960 together whenever I was off duty. I took him to Midnight Mass, hoping for a miracle. The whole occasion was ruined by Irish lads, who arrived late and drunk, and sang the carols in a key no one had heard of before or since.

I wrote to my parents to tell them that I had met someone, that our relationship was 'serious' but that he was not a Catholic. My mother usually wrote, but this time the reply came from my father. I was to finish with this 'nonsense', complete my training and return home to do my midwifery. I then wrote to say that I would bring him home to meet them, but the reply from my father was that that was unacceptable and they would not meet him. I finished my training, was successful in my final examinations and was put on the General Nursing Council Register in April 1962 under the category "General Nurse". I was now a State Registered Nurse and it was time to think about what to do next, apart from getting married against my parents' wishes.

I had enjoyed my time on the surgical wards and the time spent in the theatre observing operations. Surgery fascinated me so I decided to do a post-graduate theatre course in spite of some of my experiences during my student days in that area.

For example, one day a surgeon came into the operating room in his underpants, waving a pair of surgeon's green trousers. As the student nurses were responsible for setting out the theatre attire, he yelled at me 'Do you know Westminster Abbey?' to which I replied 'Yes'. Then he shouted, 'Has it got a ballroom?' to which I replied 'No'. 'Well, it is like these trousers, no ball-room either!' Little did I know then that I would get to know Westminster Abbey very well in my future career.

I applied to Charing Cross Hospital, which was then in Chandos Street, off the Strand in the centre of London. It is now a police station. I was accepted and left Whipps Cross to start the course in July 1962. My nursing colleagues knew that I wanted to marry Bob and were totally disapproving. Apart from one, I never heard from any of them again. I consoled myself that I would have behaved in the same way, if it had been one of them who was going to marry a non-Catholic. It was viewed as a betrayal of our religion and our culture.

I had not long started my theatre course when my parents arrived in London and hoped that they could persuade me to go home. I refused to go. I begged them to meet Bob as I hoped that might help the situation. It only made things worse. He laid down the law to my parents that I was twenty-one, he was determined to marry me and that it would not be in the Catholic Church. Years later my father admitted to me that he wished he had thrown him in the Thames. On parting, my weeping parents pressured me not to marry him and my father said to me 'He is a hard, hard man. You have not been brought up to be able to cope with this kind of person and you will regret it'. These words were to come back to me in the years that followed.

I was aware that my parents would have discussed my situation with the priests at home. It was no surprise, therefore, to receive a letter from a priest who was a family friend. He harangued me for the stress I was causing my parents and threatened that if the marriage went ahead, I would be excommunicated from the Church and would not be entitled to receive the sacraments, i.e. confession and communion. He pointed out that I was a disgrace to the family.

With hindsight, my parents might have handled it differently but the all-powerful Catholic Church's advice and guidance were always followed. After the visit to London, my father wrote to say that if I married Bob, they did not wish to see me again. We married in December 1962 and so began fourteen years of isolation from my family.

CHARING CROSS HOSPITAL

My theatre course was an interesting experience. At that time, surgeons were on a level with God and we, as nurses, were definitely the handmaidens, obedient and subservient. One of the orthopaedic surgeons, who drove a Rolls Royce and lived in Hertfordshire, was an example of the arrogance that abounded at that time. He would drive into Charing Cross Hospital, but if unable to park his car, he would drive back home and get the train into London. There was no regard for the patient who was in the anaesthetic room and the theatre staff who were ready to start the operating list. He refused to make his initial journey by train so to prevent the situation continuing, a theatre porter would be dispatched to stand on the street and keep a parking space and if necessary, lie down in the street.

As the course progressed, I gained experience of assisting at the operating table by scrubbing up with the experienced theatre nurse and observing her as she assisted the surgeon. The medical students sat in the gallery overlooking the theatre with the surgeon bellowing up at them to tell them what he was doing as he operated. There was no sophisticated equipment for teaching as there is today.

One day, the professor of surgery was performing (we do not call them "theatres" for nothing). I was observing the theatre sister assisting in a major operation. The professor asked for a certain retractor to hold the wound open. The sister, who was four foot nothing, pulled herself up to her full height and declared: 'I do not have it' The professor went red and yelled: 'Where is it?' 'It is up in the gallery where you threw it last week'. The puce-faced professor screamed 'Get out of my theatre!' Off she went and I went to follow her but he shouted: 'You stay here and take my list!'. So I, who had little idea of what I was doing, was left to take the cases.

We can all see the funny side of this but, of course, it was not at all funny. It showed a total lack of respect and unity of purpose. More importantly, it put patients at a tremendous risk in what was an unsafe situation. It showed up the fact that there was a total lack of respect between disciplines.

Theatre nursing at that time, in the early 1960s, involved making gauze swabs, packing drums with dressings sterilising drapes and gowns in autoclaves. Instruments were boiled for three minutes in special boilers.

The course was supposed to provide us with a series of lectures on such issues as infection control, anaesthetics and surgery, but we never received any lectures. We learned on the job. We were a way of recruiting theatre staff, of which there was a shortage. It was some years later that the Joint Board of Clinical Nursing Studies was set up to monitor the content of all post-graduate courses. Theatre nursing was a form of nursing that you either loved or hated. I loved it and decided that I wished to continue to do it.

ST MARY'S HOSPITAL, PADDINGTON

On completion of my theatre course, I decided to be bold and apply for a sister's post. I was accepted at Lindo Wing at St Mary's Hospital, Paddington. This was the private wing and proved to be another interesting experience. An eccentric, Sister Peat, ran the private theatre. She ran around, never walked, in white noisy open sandals.

One of the surgeons was Arthur Dickson Wright, whose famous daughter, Clarissa, admitted in her autobiography that he was an alcoholic. He was strange and would arrive hours later than the time he was booked to operate. One day, when he was very late and we had been waiting for him, trolleys set up and staff hanging around, Sister Peat decided she had had enough.

As he came into the theatre, she appeared and pulled the drapes from the trolley, sending instruments flying all over the place. She yelled at him 'We have waited hours for you, now go back into the surgeons' room and wait for us to get ready!' This involved re-sterilising the instruments and setting up the trolleys again. We went off duty very late but we were glad she had made a stand.

I also had the pleasure of working with Sir Arthur Porritt, of Olympic fame, who was a real gentleman. Another was Sir Williamson Noble, who designed many of the instruments used in eye surgery. He was a very old man at the time and we had to stop his hands from shaking when he was suturing. When I asked him why he had not retired, he informed me that having paid for his own children to go to university, he was now paying for his grandchildren, of whom there were many.

There was rivalry between anaesthetists who vied to anaesthetise for the surgeons so as to get the fees for the case. There were two who hated each other. This was portrayed in the suggestion book in the surgeons' room. An entry from one of the anaesthetists requested soft toilet paper in the surgeons' toilet and written under it was 'please can it be pink?' Another entry was a request for iced fruit juice during the hot weather which had the addition of 'please can we have some hot weather?'.

In the sixties there was no payment for being on call for emergencies, and if you were called out, you still reported for duty the next morning at the usual time. Looking back, it was exploitation, but at that time it was part of the job of being a theatre nurse. On return to duty after a week's holiday, I was put on night duty for three months. This happened to all of us who got married while post-graduate students as the matron, a spinster, did not approve.

Bob and I had been living in a rented flat on Clapham Common and decided to buy a maisonette in Bromley in Kent. I managed to draw out my superannuation in between jobs to use as a deposit. I applied for and got a sister's post at Bromley Hospital while Bob worked at the Central Office of Information in London. His real passion was swimming and he had always wanted to be a sports reporter. To follow his ambition he worked as a freelance for a newspaper as a swimming reporter. This involved attending swimming galas throughout the UK, mostly at weekends, and sometimes I accompanied him, if I was off duty.

BROMLEY HOSPITAL

I started as a theatre sister in 1963 at Bromley Hospital. It was a small general hospital. There were two operating theatres with a room in between used for laying up trolleys. This room contained two water boilers to sterilise the instruments and a large sink in which the instruments were washed before going back in the boilers. There was a small recovery room and in another room glass syringes and needles were sterilised in a hot air oven. Suturing materials came in glass phials and were stored in antiseptic. Suturing needles, scalpel blades and other sharp instruments were sterilised in dishes of antiseptic. Weekends were spent washing walls and ceilings, changing the antiseptic in the trays and dealing with emergencies.

During the 1960s and 70s major changes took place in sterilising methods, surgical procedures, theatre techniques, infection control and theatre staffing. It was an exciting time to be a theatre sister and I remained in theatre nursing for fifteen years.

Eventually all swabs and dressings were packed and autoclaved in a central area called the Central Sterile Supply Department (CSSD) and were supplied to all wards and departments. It was in Scotland, in the late 1960s, that the Procedure Pack Service was introduced. It was a joint venture between Smith and Nephew, Johnson & Johnson and the South East Scotland Regional Hospital Board. It was a commercial venture that meant that gamma irradiated standardised packs were supplied to hospitals by the firms. A great deal of debate and argument took place before agreement on standardisation was reached as to the content of each pack. This was the beginning of the commercialisation of many products seen in health care today and continued with the introduction of disposables such as drapes, gowns and gloves.

Then in 1963, the Bowie-Dick test, named after the microbiologists, J.H. Bowie and J. Dick, was introduced. This was to revolutionise theatre techniques in that the pre-set tray system was developed and was eventually used in all theatres. The pre-set tray system meant that all instruments, drapes and swabs were in the one tray, and a special tray was developed for all operations, with supplementary packs available when necessary. The unit involved in the pre-tray system became known as the Theatre Sterile Supply Unit (TSSU) and, to begin with, was attached to each suite of theatres, now standalone units off site.

When I joined the staff of Bromley Hospital in 1963 I was employed as a theatre sister. I was promoted to theatre superintendent and in 1973 I became nursing officer for theatres, one of the new titles that were introduced with the changes that occurred after the publication of the Salmon Report in 1996.

There had been talk that Bromley needed a bigger and more up-to-date hospital, and as a first phase, a new accident and emergency department was planned with two wards, two theatres, a plaster theatre and a TSSU as support. A proper recovery room equipped with piped gases and suction that would be part of the theatre suite would also be needed. Nearby would be an Intensive Care Unit (ICU). The need for this reflected the advances in surgery and anaesthetic techniques that required specialist nursing during the post-operative period.

I was involved in the planning of the theatre suite and spent many hours arguing for terrazzo flooring to be laid in the theatres, as this flooring would be easier to wash than linoleum. As always, short-term costs were put before long-term savings, but I was sure that linoleum would not stand the wear and tear and would be difficult to keep clean. With the support of the medical staff and the microbiologist, I won. Phase two of the development was to be a ward block. This was never built and Bromley Hospital is no more – it is now a housing estate.

I learned a great deal about management and leadership while in charge of theatres. It was important to value all those who worked in the area, the porters, the women who worked in the TSSU, the cleaners and the doctors and nurses. This was evident in the way the theatre Christmas party was planned. Everyone contributed a small amount of money each week from August onwards. The consultants usually gave us the booze and food was donated by most of the women. The porters ran the disco.

These parties were known in the hospital as the best parties of the season and it was not unusual to hear one of us remark, regarding the medical staff 'If he carries on like that, he will not be invited to the Christmas party', always in earshot of the offender. On the whole the medical staff were well behaved, no throwing of instruments or swearing at the nurses. We had a golden rule that we must never argue with a surgeon during an operation. However, if behaviour was unreasonable, I would see the offender in my office and point out that such behaviour was not acceptable. I remember reporting to a consultant that if his registrar continued to behave badly, then none of the nurses would scrub for him.

The other issue was the level of competence of locum registrars who wanted to take on emergency cases above their level of competency. I had on occasion secretly telephoned the consultant to find out if he knew what was happening. He would not know, but would come to the theatre to see for himself. On more than one occasion, the patient was sent back to the ward. At other times the consultant would scrub up and oversee the operation himself.

On the whole, we all got on well with each other and some of our social life centred around the hospital pub, the Tiger's Head, which was in the hospital grounds. There were no mobile phones and the switchboard would summon the doctor on call (most lived in the hospital) by a flashing light system, a combination of colours for each house officer, which was situated at strategic points in the hospital. If we were all in the pub, the switchboard operator had a system that saved the landlord from having to answer the phone. One ring would be for the medical officer, two for the casualty officer, three for the surgical houseman and four for the theatre sister. When the phone rang, we would all start counting the rings.

It was important to listen to all members of the team when any of them came up with an idea. One student nurse asked me why we removed the ward blanket covering the patient and replaced it with a cold theatre blanket when the patient was cold and nervous. The outcome was that we waited until the patient was anaesthetised and then replaced the ward blanket with the theatre one before going into the sterile area of the operating theatre. It made me realise that a new pair of eyes can produce good ideas which are not obvious to people working within a system.

One of the matters I wanted to put right was the fact that as theatre superintendent I had no input into the selection of theatre porters. Following discussions with the administrator, I was eventually allowed to sit in on the interview. However, on one occasion my interviewing skills proved inadequate. I was called to the administrator's office one day and found two strange men there who turned out to be plain-clothes police officers. They explained that Jim, whom we had employed the week before, was wanted on twenty-nine counts of robbery and they wanted to go to the theatres and arrest him. I had visions of a chase taking place round the operating theatres, so I went and got Jim to come to the office regarding a question of pay. A little while later, I saw him handcuffed to the two police officers and leaving the building.

Working in theatres made me very impatient. There was no time for what is called 'mirror management', i.e 'we are looking into it.' If there was an emergency and a theatre needed to be opened fast, then it was a case of moving staff as quickly as possible. There was no time for sitting down and discussing what we should do. I have been criticised for my impatience on many occasions.

I loved theatre nursing, but after a few years in Bromley I wanted to start a family. Eventually Bob admitted that he would not have children, he did not like children and that was that. I had come to rely on him and did as he asked. I was upset and disappointed and it was probably the first nail in the coffin of our marriage. I consoled myself that I had a profession that I enjoyed. I loved theatre nursing so I decided that the only thing to do was to forget about a family and concentrate on my career, and what a career it turned out to be.

NATN

In 1964, a visionary theatre nurse, Daisy Ayris, who was theatre superintendent in Leeds, led the way to form the National Association of Theatre Nurses (NATN). In the mid-fifties, Daisy had been invited to attend an international meeting of the Royal College of Surgeons. This prompted her to wonder whether there could be a similar organisation for theatre nurses. She wanted theatre nurses to have a common ground for meeting to discuss problems and standardise procedures for the benefit of patients, nurses and medical staff.

Theatre nursing is a branch of nursing unlike any other. Some colleagues did not believe that it was really nursing, but patients need nurses more than ever when they are unconscious and vulnerable. We were isolated behind closed doors because of the sterile area with controlled access.

Daisy won a scholarship to visit hospitals in the USA and while she was there became acquainted with an organisation, a model of which she wished to set up in the UK. The organisation was the Association of Operating Room Nurses (AORN) who had their headquarters in Denver, Colorado. On her return to the UK in 1964 she called an inaugural meeting involving interested theatre nurses, got the support of the surgeons and anaesthetists, and the NATN was born. Daisy Aryis and the National Association were to have a major impact on my life in the years ahead.

The first NATN congress was held in Harrogate in 1965 and by then there were branches all around the country. I joined the London Branch, attended the second congress in Brighton and found it of great interest. In the early days one of the medical firms with an interest in theatres organised an exhibition and we were introduced to new products on display.

It was necessary to be a member of such an organisation to keep up with all the changes taking place in the surgical arena. The branch of surgery I was particularly interested in was orthopaedics, which can be described as carpentry of bones. I had often helped out, as a teenager, in my father's business, so was well acquainted with drills and screws and the need to get the sizes right. Electric tools were introduced and we were using electric drills like those that were sold in my father's store. I would go with my father to the Cork Show where he exhibited and I would watch the power tools being demonstrated.

The long-awaited report on the Staffing and Organisation of Operating Theatres (the Lewin Report) was published in April 1971. One issue of contention was 'that operating department assistants (ODAs) should be able to take their places in the theatre team at the instrument table', i.e. as the scrub assistant / instrument nurse. The report gave the first official recognition to the technician, with the recommendation that two grades should be set up, with the titles of operating department assistant (ODA) and senior operating department assistant (SODA). The idea that the ODA could scrub up was sacrilege to many theatre nurses and that the SODA could manage an operating suite was even more sacrilege. The report was seen as a take-over bid and there was anger and frustration among many theatre nurses as the Report recommended that, with technicians scrubbing up, 'a situation is established where nurses and ODAs at appropriate level are interchangeable'.

This grade (ODA) had previously been called theatre technicians and their work was mainly helping the anaesthetist in the anaesthetic room. The need for the technician was obvious, as the anaesthetic room was an area where many nurses did not like to work. More to the point, there was a shortage of theatre nurses as the amount of time spent by student nurses in the theatre during training had been cut and in some cases they did not spend any time there. A new grade trained in all aspects of theatre work was needed to give the surgeon, as well as the anaesthetists, a better and more permanent service.

I became aware that there was a similar grade to that envisaged in the Lewin Report, called Operating Room Technician (ORT), working in the USA. I decided that I would like to investigate the training and role of this grade and find out whether there were lessons to be learnt from a visit to the USA as the Lewin Report had been accepted and the staffing of theatres would change in the future.

In 1969, the Theatre Nursing Education and Research Fellowship Fund was set up, thanks to a generous donation by the medical products group of the 3M Company. In 1971, I decided to apply for a grant. My application was an investigation into 'The training and function integration of the nurse and allied personnel in the operating theatre'. I was interviewed and was asked to first of all look at the situation in Britain and then to submit a fresh application the following year with a view to visiting the USA.

My grant of £50 allowed me to visit ten sites in all, and took in Wales, Scotland and England. Looking back, it is hard to imagine how I managed on £50, but I was given accommodation and meals everywhere. As in Accident and Emergency departments where nurses become friendly with policemen, so also in theatres, nurses become friendly with medical representatives, and I was met off trains and transferred to my destination by the reps. This would not be acceptable in today's world.

The length of time I spent in each hospital varied as I probed and studied the courses available to theatre technicians and watched them at work. I also drew comparisons between current training and that which would be needed for the ODA if the Lewin Report recommendations were implemented. All of the courses studied were based on the course set up by the Institute of Theatre Technicians (IOTT) that ran for two years and was used by two-thirds of the hospitals visited. In Scotland and Wales there was no link with the IOTT syllabus. Everywhere lectures were variable and training was mostly on the job.

With regard to training, I concluded that one national training programme was required, involving all aspects of theatre technique. Post-graduate courses should be available in specialised fields such as orthopaedic surgery, intensive care units, renal units and CSSD/TSSU departments, thus widening the field of work for the qualified technician.

Selected hospitals with the facilities should be allocated money to run these courses. The trainee should be supernumerary for the first year of a two-year course. This would prevent the trainee being used as an extra pair of hands as had been the case with many post-graduate theatre nurse courses. Clinical instructors would be vital for in-service training. This must be a theatre sister or senior technician trained in teaching. I found duplication of lectures and concluded that with efficient organisation and management, nurses and technicians could be combined in training for some aspects of theatre training that would hopefully lead to better working relationships.

With regard to integration, opinions varied widely and no apparent thought had been given to the implementation of the report. This long-awaited report was published six months before I started my study tour, yet the people who had read it in full and studied the implications were few.

All had read the sentence, 'that the Operating Department Assistant should be able to take his place in the theatre team at the instrument table'. Very few had read Paragraph 94 on assimilation. This recommended 'high standards' for the new grade and further training for existing grades with a view to later assimilation.

One thought-provoking comment was made by an anaesthetist who felt strongly that the nurse must be kept in the theatre. He put the following viewpoint: 'Theatres were in danger of becoming experimental laboratories. For example, the increase in the number of abortions and the spina bifida cases are of constant concern to the nurses, who are aware of the problems because of their training. A look or a tone of voice conveyed by the scrub nurse tells the surgeon where to draw the line in experimental surgery'.

The nursing and medical staff can communicate on the same level regarding moral issues. Due to their background training, they have surgery in perspective. The theatre technician should have patient contact by working on the ward, but a nurse should always be in charge. The nurse is the humanising element in the theatre.

The nursing staff on the whole opposed the Lewin Report. There was genuine fear that it would lead to non-nurses eventually running operating theatres. This, they felt, would bring about a lowering of standards and a lack of communication with other departments. However, the nurses' fear was of the grade of technician, as at that time nurses not involved in theatre work felt that such work did not require nurses, but it would be better if a nurse were in charge. The nurses recognised the need for technicians so far as anaesthetic room work was concerned, but felt that they should remain there. This was the opinion especially where there was no shortage of staff.

With regard to the surgeons, opinions varied widely and no apparent thought was given to the implementation of the Report. One issue the surgeons were united on was that a nurse should always be in charge of the theatre. The legal aspects of the drawing-up of drugs and swab checking would have to be changed if the Lewin Report were to be fully implemented. At that time the anaesthetist took responsibility for technicians drawing-up drugs, causing anxiety among the nurses in charge of theatres.

The report of my investigations was well received and, as requested, in 1972 I reapplied to continue the subject by investigating the situation in the USA. I was successful and went about planning my study tour. I had received a list of where the operating room technicians (ORTs) were trained and chose a selection of hospitals, one vocational school and one college to visit. Those chosen were sometimes based on where I had contacts, as my award was only £350 and I wanted to produce a comprehensive report that involved various parts of the States. I also wanted to see as much of the country as I could, as I did not think I would have another opportunity to visit. My employing authority, the Bromley Group Management Committee, was very helpful and generous and allowed me eight weeks study leave, to which I added three weeks annual leave.

Helping at the Cork Show where her father exhibited, June 1956

St Vincent's Convent

The school of 1958 (taken November 1958)

Christmas at Whipps Cross 1958.
Mary is second from the left wearing the jaunty hat

Looking at equipment with the principal and chairman of the
Operating Room Technicians College, Boston, June 1972

Exchanging views with the operating room personnel,
Southern Baptist Hospital, August 1972

Plaque presented by NATN to AORN, May 1976.
The plaque was designed by Leslie, Mary's husband.

Presenting the plaque to the AORN president Sylvia Doyle, Miami 1976

Group leaving for the AORN Congress in 1976. Mary (centre) is holding the plaque to be presented to the AORN from NATN

Group leaving for the AORN Congress in New Orleans, May 1978

Opening ceremony, Nigerian Nurses Congress, Lagos, March 1977

Giving the after dinner speech at the
Nigerian Nurses Congress, Lagos, March 1977

Outside the first NATN headquarters, October 1977. President Professor Michael Vickers, centre, Mary on his left, with other council members.

Students arriving by Brighton Health Authority
coach for lunch at Mary's home, March 1990

Mary (far left) and Leslie (next to her) entertaining
American students at home in their garden, March 1990

Congratulating students at the presentation of awards to Faculty of Health and Social Work students at Anglia Polytechnic (now Anglia Ruskin University), October 1991

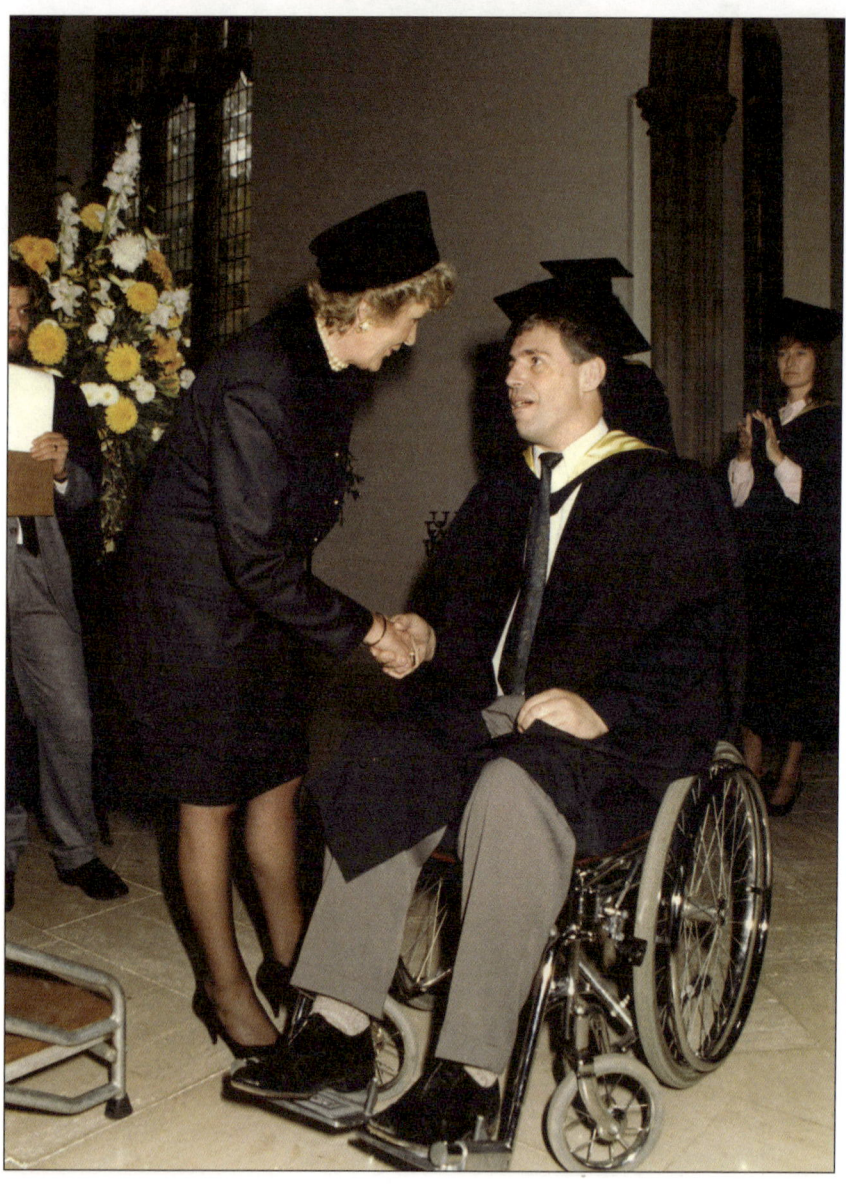

Her Majesty the Queen opening the refurbished
King Edward VII Hospital, Windsor, November 2000

Investiture: Her Majesty the Queen appointing Mary CBE, 16 November 2010

Procession of the lamp at the Florence Nightingale Commemoration Service

Escort to the book of remembrance at the
Florence Nightingale Commemoration Service

Reading a poem at the East Wellow service for Florence Nightingale, May 2010

Gathered for prayers after the service at St Margaret's, East Wellow, at the tomb of Florence Nightingale and her family, May 2010

The Most Reverend Dr Desmond Tutu, Archbishop Emeritus
of Cape Town, meets nurses at the Centenary Commemoration Service
at Westminster Abbey on 12 May 2010

Meeting the then Secretary of State for Health, Andrew Lansley,
at Mary's farewell reception, Westminster Abbey, 2010

VISIT TO THE USA 1972

I had a cousin in Boston. She arranged for me to spend my first three weeks at the Massachusetts General Hospital in Boston as well as smaller hospitals linked to the vocational school nearby. This allowed me to get acclimatised to the American health care system as I pestered my cousin with lots of questions. At that time I was called a theatre superintendent, but my cousin pointed out to me that in the USA this was a janitor in a cinema. I immediately became an operating room (OR) supervisor.

My next port of call was the famous Johns Hopkins University Hospital in Baltimore. A friend had an aunt who lived there and kindly agreed to put me up for a week. This was not long after the race riots in Baltimore and many of the white population had moved out to the suburbs. This was where the aunt lived and it meant that I had to travel by bus into Johns Hopkins early in the morning. I was the only white person on the bus, a new experience for me. Most white people went everywhere by car.

From Baltimore I flew to San Francisco, where the only nurse who kept in touch with me from my student days now lived with her husband. I wanted to spend some time at Stanford University Hospital at Palo Alto, but did not realise that it was some miles away, so I had to get up at the crack of dawn and get a Greyhound bus there and back every day. It was fascinating as the cloud remained over San Francisco. As we drove out of the city every morning, we could see the sun shining in the distance. On the way back, we left the sunshine behind when approaching the city as the cloud descended.

From there I went to Denver, Colorado and visited hospitals as well as the AORN HQ located there. I also met the President of the Association of Operating Room Technicians (AORT), a newly formed association. From Denver I went to New Orleans to the Southern Baptist Hospital and then back to the east coast where I visited hospitals in New York and New Jersey.

At the AORN I learned a lot from the personnel on how they ran their organisation, little realising how useful it would be in the years ahead.

USA Healthcare System

To begin with, it was necessary for me to get in touch with the 'American scene' at that time, which was different in many ways from what I was used to in Britain. Hospitals were either State or privately owned. Many of the large private hospitals had divisions that catered for the sector unable to pay for private medical care. A scheme called 'Medicare' allowed for almost free medical care for anyone over 65 years. Those who could afford it insured against illness and lower income groups received free medical care in the State hospitals. Many firms and industries offered their employees full or part medical insurance and some hospitals offered their staff the same bonus.

Hospital bills were rendered weekly and sent to the patient's room. Bills had to be paid as rendered and all current charges settled at the time of discharge. Hospital costs were high and climbing higher. There was much criticism of the cost of medical care and many felt a health service similar to Britain's was necessary. It was hoped that this would be launched within the next ten years, i.e. before 1982. As we are now aware, the Clinton administration failed to do this, and President Obama has been struggling to bring in a fairer system against fierce opposition. Naturally I was questioned about the British system and was asked to give a talk on it at several of the hospitals. I fully supported our system, and still do. The request for a credit card on admission to the emergency room was alien to me and filled me with dread. However, it should be stressed that no one was ever refused treatment.

In the main, operating theatres were set in one block, comprising in some hospitals up to 32 rooms. This planning allows for easy running of the suite. Most operating theatres did not have anaesthetic rooms or laying-up areas. All anaesthetic equipment and other instrumentation was ready in the operating room where the patient was put on the operating table and then anaesthetised. From the patient viewpoint, I felt the amount of equipment rather alarming, i.e. sterile trolleys of instruments, anaesthetic machines and monitors. This was the situation in the 1970s, but with the increase in technology, induction rooms have been introduced in many OR suites.

There was one list each day that began between 0730 and 0800 hours and finished by 1500 hours. The delay between cases was usually twenty minutes and there was only one list per day in each theatre, thus the ratio of theatres to surgical beds far exceeded that in the UK.

As in the UK at that time, there were two grades of nurses, the practical nurse who was the equivalent of the British state enrolled nurse, and the registered nurse (the former is now obsolete). In the USA, the registered nurse had to graduate from a school of nursing approved by the State Board for nursing and to pass a State Board examination. On the whole, the registered nurse's training was similar to my training at the time of my visit. However, I became aware that the traditional system of nurse training had been on the decline since 1965. At that time a paper on nursing education from the American Nurses Association (ANA) stated: 'The education for all those who are licensed to practice nursing should take place in institutions of higher education'.

This resulted in associate degree programmes and baccalaureate programmes both being based in colleges. There was much criticism of the graduate nurse from the college course because of her lack of practical experience. Many student nurses worked as nursing aides during vacations. This criticism tended to come from the older nurses and many doctors, especially those from countries which had not embarked on this system of training. History repeated itself in the UK with the introduction of Project 2000 in 1991, when nursing education was moved into universities and the apprentice type of training was discontinued. I agreed with the move to higher education but was concerned at how academia seemed to take over and it was forgotten that nursing was fundamentally a practical profession.

Theatre Staffing

At the time of my study, 43 theatre technicians were in charge of theatres in the USA, mostly in small hospitals. There was concern that this number would increase because of the lack of theatre experience in the student nurses' training programmes. A week was the most time that students spent in theatres during their course. There was concern that students were being told that theatre work was below their qualifications and was only fit for theatre technicians. In the whole of the USA there were just seven post-graduate courses available to qualified nurses. Many were discontinued after technician courses started. Most hospitals had in-service training programmes for new staff, and an instructor was employed for this role. Orientation programmes were always arranged for all grades of staff that participated in these together, thus saving time and staff as well as helping integration.

It was difficult to analyse the shortage of theatre nurses throughout the USA as the situation varied from state to state. In certain hospitals, theatres were closed because it was against hospital policy to run an operating theatre without a nurse. In these hospitals there was a surplus of trained technicians.

I had come to study theatre technicians with regard to training and function integration, known in the USA as the Operating Room Technician

(ORT). In a country the size of the USA, it was impossible to visit every institution running a technician course, but I learned a lot from the AORN and especially from Jerry Peers, who was in charge at that time.

In about 1960, working with the American College of Surgeons, the American Hospitals Association, and the National League of Nurses, the AORN was acutely aware of the lack of consistency in training, utilization and standards of the ORT. A committee was set up to investigate this. In 1967, an instruction manual was written by four skilled operating theatre superintendents, outlining a formal course that would assure a quality standardized course.

In 1968, the AORN voted to create an associated organization, and in 1969 the new organization called the Association of Operating Room Technicians (AORT) was formed. The educational division of AORN then began the evaluation of courses for technicians. Eventually AORT set up a system of certification to achieve high standards. It was necessary to pass an examination set by AORT to gain certification.

Technician training was of two kinds. One was organised by the hospital and the other by a college. High school education was a necessity for entrance to most courses, whether hospital- or college-based. The duration of the hospital-based course was one year, while the college-based course visited was one school year and included clinical experience in affiliated local hospitals.

Having looked at the situation in the USA, I endorsed the previous recommendation that I made after my British study, that there be one national training programme for ODAs involving all aspects of theatre technique. I felt that guidelines by AORN and certification had done much to standardise the technician training programmes in the USA. In the UK, we were in a position to organise one unified course and a series of national examinations. The Institute of Theatre Technicians examination in the UK should lead to national certification, implying that the technicians would be examined, tested and compared on a national basis.

I heard many views on the integration of nurses and technicians during my visits to hospitals and training institutions. There was concern that eventually there would be no nurses in the ORs of the future. Finance being of major importance in the USA health system, administrators were therefore welcoming technicians as their salaries were only two thirds of a nurse's, thus saving money. However, there are no set salary scales as in the UK, so salaries can be negotiated. In the USA, legal aspects vary from state to state and laws and rules vary from hospital to hospital. However, the law on the drawing-up of drugs was adhered to, i.e. technicians were not allowed to draw-up or give drugs, at least not in the hospitals I visited. Rules on swab checking called for a nurse to participate in every swab count but I was told that this was not always adhered to. So the legal system would have to change if there were only technicians in ORs.

Medical staff were not over-concerned with the grade of staff in the theatre, but all felt a nurse should be in charge. They were more concerned with having enough staff to assist them to operate. The American College of Surgeons had passed a resolution that a nurse should always be in charge of the OR. The surgeons were content with the performance of the technicians as scrub assistants. Many viewed them only in this function, with the nurse as a circulator. It was felt, and rightly so, that the role of the circulating nurse was of greater importance than the scrubbing role.

Many and varied opinions on integration were produced by the nursing staff. Generally, the younger and newly qualified nurse was much more likely to accept the technician than the older nurse. Some admitted that as a scrub assistant, the technician was superior to the nurse. The need for the technician was admitted by many nurses, but there was bitterness because of the absence of theatre training in the student nurses' curriculum. In many hospitals, there was friction between the nurses and technicians when technicians were first employed, but as technicians proved themselves useful members of the team because of their excellent training, they were gradually accepted.

In hospitals where the technician was employed as a scrub assistant only, many nurses resented the fact that they never had an opportunity to scrub. And yet, because of the laws and rules of the hospital, they were required as circulator/runner to sign for swab counts, and fetch and administer medication when necessary. It was also the nurse's responsibility to fill in forms listing the sutures, prosthetics etc. that were used. These would be costed and met by the patient as part of the surgical fee. In a situation where a technician was scrubbed and another running in the same room, the nurse supervising the area resented the responsibility of signing for swab counts she had not witnessed. There were not enough nurses to run the ORs according to the rules.

On integration, I concluded that, with selective recruitment and proper training, it would be possible to integrate the nurse and the technician in the working situation. If we could not get nurses coming into theatre work in sufficient numbers, we had to accept the technician and ensure that the training was of a standard that would provide safe care of the surgical patient. However, it would also be necessary to ensure that student nurses were exposed to what theatre nursing was about if we wanted to keep nurses in the theatre as well.

The following, expressed by a colleague in the USA, summed up my own feelings at the time. 'The person who performs the duties in the theatre must be the most qualified, most competent person we can get. What his/her title is, nurse or technician, is not important. What is important is that he/she gives safe patient care with a thorough knowledge and understanding of the responsibilities involved'.

Touring the States

Of course, my study tour was not all work and no play. Everywhere I went, my hosts were wonderfully generous in ensuring that I enjoyed their country. One of the delights was the range of different food which I had not come across before. I enjoyed pastrami on rye (bread) in New York, clam chowder in Boston, large steaks in Denver and oysters in New Orleans.

I went sailing off the coast of New Jersey and walked on the beach in San Francisco when the sun shone for the first time in my week-long visit. I visited a ranch outside Denver and drove to a model outpost up in the hills where you could imagine scenes from the cowboy films. I went to the top of the Empire State Building and went on a cruise around Staten Island, New York. After dinner one evening in Baltimore, when sitting in the garden having another glass of wine, I noticed little lights flashing nearby. I thought the wine had gone to my head but it was fireflies, insects I had never even heard of.

At the time of my study tour New York and Newark were not as safe as they are today. However, I enjoyed walking around New York, much to the consternation of some of my contacts there, medical firm representatives in particular. One evening I walked to the Lincoln Centre in the hope of seeing 'A Little Night Music' starring Hermione Gingold and Glynis Johns. I managed to get a ticket and it was most enjoyable. Another time I took a bus through Harlem as I had heard a lot about the area. One night while studying at the hospital in Newark, New Jersey, I went into New York to meet some friends. I tried to get a taxi back to Newark rather late at night, but the first few I approached refused to take me because it was considered a very dangerous area. Eventually one agreed, but warned me to lock my doors in the back of the cab. When we got to the residence of the hospital he told me that he would keep his headlights on and I should run as fast as I could to the door of the residency.

When I related all this to my USA contacts in conversation, they were concerned for my safety and thought I was crazy to take risks that they considered dangerous. When I finally got on the plane home, I am sure they breathed a sigh of relief.

Then and now

It is now over forty years since I investigated the staffing of operating theatres and the integration of nurses and technicians in them. Following the publication of the Lewin Report in 1971, the headline in the nursing press was that there would be no nurses in the operating theatre in ten years. Some colleagues in the USA made the same prediction. In return I wrote an article entitled 'Do not write our epitaph!'. So was the headline true, or was I right to entitle the article as I did? There have been many changes since then, not only in operating theatres but also in the whole of healthcare.

I am pleased to report that there are still nurses in theatres both in the USA and the UK. There is no longer a clinical placement of six weeks for student nurses within the theatre area either here or in the USA. This is not surprising considering the changes (in technology, interventions and the increased number of procedures and treatments available today) that student nurses have to learn about. Exposure to theatres mainly occurs as part of a surgical experience when the student accompanies the patient through the process of pre-operative, inter-operative and post-operative care. To me, theatre nursing is a fascinating part of patient care and it is no wonder that some students get the bug and decide that theatre nursing is what they would like to do. With regard to post-graduate courses for nurses, in this country there are combined courses for nurses and technicians in theatre techniques. In the USA many postgraduate courses have the flexibility to concentrate project/papers and theses on the OR.

In both countries most technician courses are now based in universities or colleges and certification is in place. Here, there has not been an increase in the number of technicians in charge of theatres. In the States, the nurse remains in charge and it would appear that the law has not changed regarding medication and swab counts. The nurse continues to circulate. Most technicians, now called surgical technologists, are female, as they were during my study tour.

In the UK, nurses and technicians work side by side and appear to be interchangeable. Advertisements for theatre posts ask for one or the other and the vacancy is open to both grades. It would appear that there is little friction and following further training, especially in management, senior technicians are now in charge of operating theatres. Technician training has moved to universities and results in a Diploma in Health Care and most recently, a Bachelor of Science degree. The programmes are organised by the College of Operating Department Practitioners, (CODP). Operating Department Practitioner (ODP) is the new name for the theatre technician.

Major changes have occurred in the organisations leading the theatre nurses and the technicians, both here and in the USA. The NATN changed its name and its constitution in 2005 to encompass other grades involved in theatre work and is now called the Association for Peri-operative Practice (AfPP). The Association has informed me that its membership is now made up of approximately 75% nurses and 25% technicians. The technicians' organisation is now the College of Operating Department Practitioners (CODP), with links to the trade union Unison. In the USA, AORT has come out from under the umbrella of AORN, has moved its headquarters, and is now known as the Association of Surgical Technologists (AST).

So nothing remains the same, as in most aspects of health care. I did not remain the same after my study tour. I came back a much more confident person, able to stand on my own two feet having spent nearly three months making my way around a vast country. I met many different people with whom I needed to communicate and learn from their experiences. I was to witness the same changes many years later when I became Director of the Florence Nightingale Foundation and we sent scholars on study tours.

CHANGES 1972–74

I took stock of my personal life and decided that I could not stay in what had become a loveless marriage. Two things were the final straws in my decision. The first was that one of my staff, a married sister, informed me that my husband had tried to persuade her to go out with him while I was away. The second involved money. I decided to open my own bank account because until then, my husband had managed all money transactions, even though we had a joint account. I asked for money when I needed it. I reckoned that my three months' salary would have been paid into the bank during my absence. I went to the bank and asked for that money, or some of it, to be transferred to a new account in my name. The bank teller went away and then a manager appeared and asked me to come into his office. The joint account was in the red and I was embarrassed and mortified. The manager was very sympathetic and offered to open an account in my name and put £25 into it against my next salary. This convinced me that the sooner I started a new life on my own, the better.

I left everything but a few bits and pieces I wanted and, after staying with a friend for a few months, moved into a small flat that I could afford. I did not know how to tell my parents. My pride put me off contacting them. I was forced into doing so when the nursing administrator told me that I needed to change my next of kin, as my husband was no longer in that position. I decided to swallow my pride and wrote to my father to tell him what had happened. He immediately phoned me to know if I was all right and asked me if I had enough money. I decided I had to go home and face them. I looked forward to this, but at the same time I dreaded it as it was fourteen years since the split and we would all have changed in the intervening years. I eventually went unannounced, arrived at Cork Airport and phoned my father at work. He came to pick me up at the airport and we drove home to meet my mother who was waiting at the door when we got there. It was a very emotional homecoming and in the years before they died I had the chance to get back to knowing and loving them. I know of others with my background and history who went to America and Australia and never saw their parents again. Another bonus is that my family got to know Leslie, the man I would eventually marry. We had many enjoyable trips home together before they died and I will be forever thankful for those opportunities. They became very fond of Leslie and knew I was happy with him.

Now that I was on my own, I decided to work hard at my career and became involved in the NATN. I was elected Chairman of the London Branch and, as such, attended the meetings of the National Executive. This was made up of the national officers and the chairman of each of the branches. At the April Executive in 1974, it was announced by the chairman, Jean Hudd, that the vice-chairman had had to resign and she needed a new vice-chairman until a new one could be elected at Congress in the autumn. I was sitting near Daisy Ayris who looked across at me and asked, 'You are in London and would not mind giving Jean some help, would you?'. (Jean was working at University College Hospital in London.) Before I could reply, Daisy had shot her arm in the air to attract attention and proposed that I be the stand-in. This was accepted, mainly because Daisy was highly respected and no one would want to contradict her. But I was only 34 at the time and the three National Chairmen before me had all been much older. I was seen by some as a bit of an upstart, despite my work on theatre staffing, and I was the first not to come from a teaching hospital background. But at this stage I was only a stand-in as the vice-chairman.

SOUTH AFRICA

In May 1975, because of my work on theatre staffing and as acting vice-chairman, I was invited to a conference in South Africa to talk about my findings. Theatres there did not have technicians as members of staff and wanted to find out if this grade could replace theatre nurses. Johnson & Johnson, who were to look after me during my visit, sponsored me. I was delighted to be going and spent many hours preparing a paper that would be helpful to my hosts. I did not spend much time thinking of the political situation in South Africa. I was, when I look back, politically naïve. My sponsors sent their company's Rolls Royce to Bromley Hospital to take me to the airport and held a small reception there to send me on my way. This was luxury I had never known.

The purpose of my visit was to read a paper on 'The Introduction and Training of Technical Theatre Assistants in British and American Hospitals' at the Transvaal Theatre Nurses Congress in Johannesburg. The theme of the congress was 'Continuing Education', a subject very dear to me. Our colleagues in South Africa, who were thinking of introducing a new grade of theatre staff, wished to learn from the experience of others.

After the Congress I visited hospitals in the Transvaal, Natal and the Cape Province on a tour organised by the Transvaal theatre nurses and nursing organisations in each area. I received a warm welcome everywhere and made many new friends. But as a guest in their country, I had to watch my Ps and Qs when it came to apartheid.

With every theatre nurse congress, the social side is not lacking and this was no exception. Although the theme was 'Continuing Education', I am not sure whether the organising committee intended our 'education' on a wide range of topics, to continue into the early hours of the morning ... but it did.

The Congress was well organized and the topics were interesting and stimulating. The theme of the first day was 'Infection Control' and the speakers covered many aspects of this subject. A surgeon stressed the importance of correct theatre design and was supported by a consultant in hospital design, using the architectural point of view. The latter showed why closer contact between the architectural and theatre professions at the earliest possible design stage is of the utmost importance in attaining an ideal final result. Although I was attending a congress many hundreds of miles from home, it all sounded rather familiar. Two senior nurses talking

43

on 'Theatre discipline in relation to infection control and in-service training' took up the remainder of this session; the importance of both for all grades of staff was stressed.

In the afternoon, an infection control officer spoke on 'The structure and value of infection control committees in hospitals', which was followed by an interesting talk on 'standardisation' by Miss Elise Michau, chief matron at the Cape Department of Hospital Services. Elise, who was an associate member of NATN, had visited Britain the year before to investigate CSSD and TSSU here in the UK. Mr. D. Honey, who was a hospital design consultant and an ex-nurse, gave some practical suggestions for TSSU. He had been working closely with South African nurse Pat Visser in setting up a large CSSD/TSSU complex in the Windhoek State Hospital in southwest Africa under challenging circumstances. Pat had been a member of the London branch of NATN while she was working at Roehampton Hospital a few years earlier.

The morning session on the second day came under the heading 'Is there a place in the operating theatre of South Africa for a new category of personnel'? and this was where I said my piece. The theatre technician, however, was not the only category of personnel under review. There was also a panel to discuss the nurse anaesthetist. There was a great shortage of anaesthetists in South Africa and a solution to the problem was being sought, The Ministry of Health gave anaesthetic assistants official approval in South Africa in September 1974. The educational requirement to train for this new post was South African matriculation level, equivalent to our O-levels. Under the legislation, after two years training in a provincial hospital, these anaesthetic assistants would be allowed to administer anaesthetics under the supervision of a 'medical' anaesthetist. The Registered Nurse was exempt from one year of training.

The two professors of anaesthesia on the panel, Professor Ginsberg and Professor Van Hasselt, were against the whole idea of anaesthetic assistants. The South African Society of Anaesthetists had rejected the new legislation and one wondered how this was passed.

The two professors were not in agreement about the nurse anaesthetist. Professor Van Hasselt, in calling for a re-examination of all the partners in the health services, felt that highly skilled nurses should do special work, such as administer anaesthetics under the supervision of specialists. Professor Ginsberg was worried about the danger to patients if anaesthetics were given by other than qualified medical staff, even though nurse anaesthetists had been in existence in America and Sweden for many years. She felt the problem could be alleviated by the introduction of anaesthetic nurses to assist anaesthetists but that they should not replace them.

Dr. John Inkster, head of the department of anaesthetists at the Sick Children's Hospital in Newcastle upon Tyne, then gave an excellent talk on the duties of the anaesthetic nurse in Britain, illustrated by slides showing his nurses at work.

I was next on the programme and outlined the training of technicians in Britain and America and the integration that had taken place in both countries. I hoped my talk helped to identify problems and avoid pitfalls with which we had had to deal.

Miss R. J. du Plessis, deputy executive director of the South African Nursing Association gave the South African standpoint on a new grade of theatre staff. The message came over loud and clear. The technician was not wanted and in fact was not needed in South Africa. I began to wonder what I was doing there. The number of State Registered and State Enrolled Nurses was quoted. During the discussion that followed, a question from the floor challenged these numbers stating that all those registered were not in practice, especially as many South African nurses do not work after marriage. (How lucky can you get?) After further discussion, it became clear that the numbers quoted included black and white nurses and in fact I was witnessing a strange paradox of apartheid. White nurses were allowed to treat coloured patients, but coloured nurses might not treat white patients. So apartheid created an artificial shortage of nurses for white patients.

The Congress was attended only by white nurses, a request to have it multi-racial having been turned down by the Government.

'Preparation for Disaster' was the topic of the afternoon. Mrs. S. Kalter, head nurse of operating theatres at Chaim Sheba Medical Center, Israel, gave an excellent talk on Operating Theatre Management in wartime. Her slides took us to the front lines and showed operating theatres that could be erected in five minutes, and the variety of surgery dealt with. When talking together later, she was adamant that theatre technicians are 'not on' in her situation. 'Why not?' I asked. She said that she had trained forty technicians to function at the front line to replace theatre nurses, as she felt the work was very stressful for girls. However, after qualifying, the technicians decided to do medicine. So the nurses were back manning the theatres at the front, and Mrs. Kalter's only consolation was that she had increased the number of medical personnel available to the injured troops.

Medico-legal aspects were discussed at the final session. This was a worrying topic for all theatre nurses, but it was of vital importance to South African theatre nurses as they were solely responsible for swab counts. Many questions on this topic as well as those on consent forms were put to the panel, which consisted of a chief nursing officer, a member of the Medical and Dental Council and an advocate of the law. An amusing story was told to answer the question. 'What does the theatre nurse do when a surgeon is about to perform an operation of which, in her opinion he is not capable?' Once in such a situation in South Africa, a nurse locked the surgeon in a cupboard and called the senior consultant.

In the afternoon, talks on two important, but vastly different, aspects of patient care were given. Dr. Inkster spoke on the care of infants during surgery. Dr. Friesen, from the USA, who was a design health care consultant, spoke on his speciality in the year 2000, 25 years forward from the time of the Congress.

The complexities of modern patient care would call for a more thoroughly planned and precisely executed effort than ever before, he claimed. In health care planning it would be necessary to have flexibility and be adaptable to the particular needs of any type of facility or institution, whatever its size. Tailoring to the requirements and goals of any country was very important.

Thus ended a very successful Congress and it was for me a great opportunity to make friends and exchange ideas. We all kept in touch for many years.

Hospitals in South Africa

The first hospital I visited was the most impressive for several reasons. It is one of the largest hospitals in the world, containing 2,500 beds; it served an entirely black population; it was originally a halfway station en route to the gold fields; it served as a rehabilitation unit for British military patients who had tuberculosis during World War II, and it is called after a Cornishman. I am referring to the world famous medical centre of Baragwaneth, (Bara) a multi-discipline general hospital or, as your feet will tell you, a series of hospitals contained in a hundred acre building complex. It lies south west of Johannesburg, and serves the sprawling dormitory satellite city of Soweto which houses 1–2 million black South Africans.

It had many physical problems, housing, feeding and treating 80 to 85 thousand inpatients per year, outpatients numbering 1,088 million per year; specimens of tissue and body fluid numbering 5,000,000 analysed each year and meals to suit dietary and ethnic requirements numbering 15,000 prepared and served each day.

Of the various departments, I was obviously most interested in the department of surgery, which contained eleven operating theatres. The volume and complexity of work undertaken was great, and included at that time up to ten aortic and mitral valve replacements every month. A new surgical wing contained five diagnostic theatres for highly sophisticated examination under general anaesthesia. Two ultra-modem intensive care units containing thirty-three beds and staffed by skilled African personnel had also opened. The dialysis unit possessed eight 'artificial kidneys'; this unit is kept open at night by urologists from Johannesburg, because the black worker faces employment difficulties if he has to attend the unit two or three mornings a week. The paediatric unit was an eye-opener into how disease varies from climate to climate and from population to population. African children's greatest killer was summer diarrhoea. Through a combination of hygiene, fluid replacement, medication and nutrition, the sting of rapid infantile death is being removed but as it was autumn in South Africa during my visit, only a small number of black babies were observed in the 'drip room'. Where possible, infants are treated as outpatients, but if admittance is needed each baby is admitted with its mother, not only for the obvious reasons but also for instruction in hygiene and nutrition.

Attached to the paediatric unit was a metabolic centre where skilled attention was given to the nutritional problems of African communities. There, nutritionists developed diets which use food readily available in the various tribal environments as well as being balanced in composition. For example, if certain proteins were not available to the ethnic group, new combinations of available food were investigated. An incredible example of this was discovered just outside the gates of Baragwaneth. In the township of Soweto, far from the sea, mothers, although unable to afford adequate meat supplies, had never in their lives tasted fish, a cheaper and appropriate alternative source of protein.

Bara Hospital had its own college of nursing and within such a wide area of experience many post-basic courses were held, including one in theatre technique and intensive care nursing. To my surprise, many of the ambulance drivers at Bara were female. They have proved more reliable than their men-folk in carrying out this responsible job. Even the male population admitted that women were spearheading the social revolution of progress among the black people. My visit and experiences at Bara were a glimpse into another world.

Johannesburg is surrounded by gold mines and I was given the opportunity of visiting one, and seeing the hospital and rehabilitation facilities available to miners. The Chamber of Mines Hospital was modern and contained a theatre suite of the three-corridor system design. Six theatre nurses, who did not believe in job demarcation lines and consequently received very high salaries, staffed the theatres. They alone provided the 24-hour service as well as the CSSD/TSSU service. This was only achievable because the number of operation cases per month was approximately 100.

The Rehabilitation Hospital was also modern and no money was spared in providing the best possible facilities for those recovering from mine injuries. They included two swimming pools, bowling alley, games room and a well-equipped occupational therapy unit. However, these were for white workers only and I did not get the opportunity to see the facilities for black workers, if there were any.

The two other hospitals visited in Johannesburg were poles apart. The General is a large provincial hospital of many years' standing, with all the problems of an old building. A new hospital to replace the General was being built outside the city and a new transplant unit would be included. There were to be thirty theatres and concern was expressed about the shortage of staff that already existed. Maybe the theatre technicians would be required after all.

The other hospital, the Brenthurst Clinic, was a splendid private clinic organized and maintained by Dr. Jack Penn, FRCS, MBE, a gifted plastic surgeon and a talented sculptor and author. I was delighted to receive a copy of Dr. Penn's latest book 'The Right to Look Human', which not only told of his unique experience in the reconstructive field, but ventured into the political arena.

Pretoria is the capital of South Africa, and when I was there I had the opportunity to discuss the future of nursing with the nursing administrators. Concern was expressed about the fragmentation of the service and we also discussed the nursing auxiliary training and assessment, now compulsory.

The next stop was Durban and in between visiting hospitals I had my first swim in the Indian Ocean. Joyce Maguire, nursing inspector of theatres for the Natal Provincial Administration, arranged this tour. Joyce had attended our congress in Bournemouth the year before my visit and she had visited hospitals in the UK. She was critical of the amount of disposables used and the wastage involved here. This may be valid in certain instances, but having visited her country the reasons became clear. In South Africa labour is cheap compared with here, and work in CSSD/TSSU provides employment for many people who would otherwise be out of work. Non-disposable syringes are still used, swabs are received untied, and in some cases abdominal packs are washed and re-sterilized.

In Durban I visited the King Edward Hospital for the black population, the Kahn Hospital for the Indian population, and Addington Hospital which is a 'mixed' hospital.

My last port of call was Cape Town, and I agree with Francis Drake that this is the most beautiful cape in the world. It is also the home of one of the world's most famous hospitals, the Groote Schur. As with every mixed hospital, the Groote Schur has duplication of services in all areas. However, in the famous research centre, black and white people work together for the future welfare of mankind and both 'colours' were involved in the first ever heart transplant.

Mr. Brian Cohen was there working on sheep, perfecting the technique for the breakthrough operation carried out a few days previously, the first fallopian tube transplant. In the Christiaan Barnard cardiac unit a heart was being transplanted from one baboon to another without removing the recipient's heart.

My visit to the Red Cross War Memorial Hospital for Children was concentrated on the burns unit and many of the pathetic sights seen there are caused by the use of paraffin for heating and cooking in the black townships. I was worried about the disappearance of the black pigmentation of the skin in some cases and wondered how acceptable the black child would be on returning to the tribe with 'patches of pink'. I was told that very often they were not accepted, just as with some tribes the birth of twins is not tolerated, and one of the babies is killed.

The Tygerburg Hospital, the last I visited, had just been completed and consisted of almost 2,000 beds. It had fifty theatres on two floors with a floor between containing rest rooms and offices. Each theatre had its own spacious scrub-room, anaesthetic room, and area for writing-up notes, forms, etc. Not all the theatres were yet in use, due to a shortage of nursing and anaesthetic staff.

The CSSD/TSSU complex was vast, had numerous autoclaves and housed two ethylene oxide sterilizers and aerators. Nursing aides/auxiliaries worked within this area under the supervision of a nurse manager.

Miss Elise Michau accompanied me on my tour of hospitals and, as is characteristic of her, allowed time for me to enjoy the delights of Cape Town. I made the journey by cable car to the top of Table Mountain to enjoy the panoramic view and, as a lover of wine, my visit to the Nederburg Wine

Farm was most enjoyable. The Cape people are very proud of their wines and I was given the opportunity to sample them.

Throughout my tour, it was obvious that there was great interest among the nurses in everything that was happening in British nursing. In fact there was still interest in anything British, and I was greatly amused at the amount of coverage given to cricket results in the newspaper, from Cardiff, Guildford. Yorkshire, you name it.

At that time the four provinces, Transvaal, Natal, Cape and Orange Free State had their own theatre groups which functioned separately, and organized Congress in turn.

Surgical firms staged an exhibition and in return sponsored visiting speakers. I hoped our relationships with South Africa theatre nurses and our exchange of participants at Congress would continue. We could do much to guide them, just as AORN helped us at the start.

The main purpose of my visit was to read a paper on technicians. From talking to people, visiting hospitals, and reading newspaper articles, I began to wonder if there would be a need to train a new grade of staff if apartheid did not exist in the field of nursing. If détente were to succeed in the future, I felt that my paper would not have been necessary. I would not complain but would be delighted that things had changed for the better for the black and ethnic populations.

Although my trip to South Africa was interesting and enjoyable, there were certain aspects that I found disturbing. I had to bite my tongue on more than one occasion. It was only when I had time to reflect on apartheid that I appreciated the full force of what the black population was suffering. I felt that the situation was hopeless and that their situation would never improve. I was extremely sad and at the same time angry and frustrated that the situation had been allowed to develop. Two gentlemen from Wellcome Laboratories whom I met on my flight home, gave an interesting dimension as to how it had happened. They told me that the British expats in South Africa had not given up their British passports so were not allowed to vote in elections there. Therefore the Afrikaners were able to bring about apartheid.

In Cape Town I had looked across at Robben Island and wondered if Nelson Mandela would remain there for the rest of his life. His release years later was a cause of joy to me and I have followed events in South Africa closely since my visit, sometimes with great expectations and at times with exasperation that a country with so many assets has not done enough for their black population.

CHAIRMAN OF NATN – FIRST YEAR

At the 1975 Conference, a new chairman was to be elected as Jean Hudd's term of office was coming to an end. I was asked if I would like my name to go forward. It would be a huge commitment and I gave it a great deal of thought. My staff encouraged me to go for it and my employers were happy for me to do so. I had a great team of staff, competent and dedicated to their work. Many were married and had moved to the area. They were well trained and some had been students who had undertaken their placement with us, had enjoyed it and decided theatre work was what they wanted to do. This was mainly due to the excellent clinical instructor for theatres, Beryl Knight (formerly Shepherd), who ensured that they learned a great deal on their placement.

Some staff had children, but we had a crèche so they were able to leave their children there during working hours. We operated like a family so if an operating list overran, one nurse would pick up another's children and look after them until Mum was off duty. In this way, we never cancelled operations. Cancellations would have been seen as failure as we realized the trauma that a cancelled operation would be for the patient and the family involved.

At this time, Leslie and I had become close and I confided in him regarding becoming chairman. He encouraged me to do so, just as he was to encourage me during the rest of my career. He became my lover, best friend, adviser, supporter and mentor, and remained so for the rest of my career. We eventually married and it was wonderful.

Leslie had been involved with NATN at the beginning. Ethicon, who helped Daisy Aryis at the start, asked Leslie, who was the design consultant who put their catalogue together at that time, to go and see Daisy about redesigning our logo. So it was through NATN that we met.

So my nomination went ahead and the citation to elect me was published in NATN News in August 1975. It stated my philosophy that nurses, by virtue of their practical experience in direct contact with patients at their most vulnerable, have a vitally important contribution to make to the advancement of medicine generally; that we needed to make sure that our voices were heard on safe patient care and avail ourselves of the ongoing process of continuing education through membership of NATN.

I was elected unopposed at the Conference in October. What followed for me over the next three years was the most exciting, most exhausting, most rewarding and most stimulating period of my career in operating theatres, if not in my whole career in nursing.

The three years consisted of visits overseas to speak at conferences and foster international relationships and learning, and visits to branches to explore the challenges facing grass roots members and to act on these. There were many meetings with other organisations on issues that were important at that time and from them various guidance was produced. There was our own conference to oversee at which I made a keynote speech at the opening ceremony.

In my first 'Letter from the Chairman', published in NATN News in January 1976, I set out my determination to increase the membership so that our educational work would be more effective. Our main objective was improvement in standards for the surgical patient. Linked to that, I wanted to concentrate on the education of all grades of theatre staff. The time spent in theatre by student nurses was being reduced. There was a need for a look at the number, location and number of theatre nurse courses for qualified nursing staff. With continuing education in mind, should we design a part-time updating course for senior theatre nurses? Should we be ambitious and practical and have joint education courses for theatre nurses and operating department assistants? I also pointed out that I needed feedback from the membership to help me address the issues in the ever-changing world of healthcare. I used the saying attributed to lots of people including Gandhi, who was quoted as saying 'These are my people, I will follow them because I am their leader'.

I am amused to read in all of the speeches I made over my three years (1976 to 1978) that I refer to cutbacks, scarce resources and the detrimental effect of re-organisations due to the NHS being a political football. Does nothing change?

One of the earliest matters to be involved with was the pollution of operating theatres by anaesthetic gases. Research had revealed that there was an increased risk of miscarriage among female theatre staff. I represented theatre nurses on a working group with the Association of Anaesthetists and the Royal College of Obstetricians. We produced guidance on scavenging devices that were attached to anaesthetic machines so that staff did not come into contact with the harmful gases. One of the other inventions at that time was the use of downward flow ventilation in the prevention of infection.

This was first introduced in orthopaedic theatres where any infection might have dire consequences for the patient.

My first trip overseas was to speak at the opening ceremony of AORN in Miami. Twenty-two members of NATN accompanied me. This reflected the many friendships that had developed with theatre nurses in the USA, some of whom had come to the NATN Conference over the years. It was a very special occasion for me and a chance to catch up with friends I had made at AORN HQ and others during my study tour in 1972. However, before I left for the USA in March 1976, I was asked to be on a panel of inquiry into an anaesthetic accident at the Westminster Hospital in London. I had to take with me reams of papers relating to the inquiry and instead of attending all the interesting lectures, I had to spend many hours reading as the inquiry was to begin the day after I returned from Miami. The one plus was that I did the reading in the sun and went swimming in the sea when I got too hot.

The 12th Congress of NATN was held in Harrogate at the end of October 1976 and was for me a daunting experience. The Mayor of Harrogate gave a reception for all the delegates and attended the opening of the Congress at which I gave the keynote address. Dr. Gerard Vaughan, MP for Reading and a Minister of Health official, opened the Congress and exhibition. The overseas visitors were the President of the Nigerian Theatre Nurses Association, the President of AORN, and the chief nursing officer of Cape Town, whom I had met in South Africa. We also had guests from Malawi and Kenya.

I started by thanking all those attending, especially the exhibitors, who put money into the Association by exhibiting although at that time the organiser, Newton Mann Ltd, had to get their share of the income for their work. There was great importance placed on the fact that it was often the theatre nurses who influenced the design and production of new products because of the close working relationships with surgeons and anaesthetists. This has waned over the years and now that there is central buying from a limited list of products, any influence has been lost. I referred to the ongoing tension between nurses and technicians but positive progress was brought about by meetings between NATN, the Institute of Theatre Technicians and the Society of Operating Department Assistants, and I was happy to report this to the membership. The Department of Health eventually sent a representative to the meetings, as there was a need to discuss the grading of the new grades of staff and the important question of how their remuneration would compare with the nursing salaries.

I finished by stressing the importance of nursing, especially in the operating theatre where unconscious patients were at their most vulnerable. There is always the need to remember that, in spite of cutbacks and mounting administration, the care of patients has to be paramount in our working lives. I have never believed in strike action by nurses.

At that time I had little experience of public speaking and I am sure I bored everyone to death, as I had not learned the need to pause and to apply emphasis on certain things. The real nightmare was giving the after dinner speech when one had to be very careful not to be risqué in any way but to make it short and let everyone get on and enjoy themselves as there was dancing to follow. Our president at the time was ill and unable to attend Congress, so our president elect, anaesthetist Dr. Michael Vickers, stood in at the last minute for which I was very grateful. Michael had a wicked sense of humour as well as being a great support and we became good friends. Another person who became a great friend was Janet King, who was the only employee of the Association. We called her the secretary but she would turn her hand to anything required without batting an eyelid and she often kept me going through thick and thin. She also had a great sense of humour and we still keep in touch.

Leslie picked me up after the Congress and drove me home. I was mentally and physically exhausted and slept the whole way home in the car. The Congress involved many late nights and meeting many people. Talking to members and getting their views informally was very important and talking to the exhibitors was vital, as without them and the revenue generated, the Congress would have suffered a great loss.

THE SHEWAN INQUIRY

In February 1975 a 26-year-old woman named Elizabeth Shewan returned from Japan, where she was teaching English, to have a routine operation at the Westminster Hospital in London. She thought that it would be safer to have treatment in her own country. Following an anaesthetic accident, she was left with severe cognitive disability. It was alleged that she had the mentality of a three year old. The inquiry into the accident became known as the Shewan Inquiry.

I flew back from the AORN Congress in Miami overnight, had a short rest and went to London that evening to meet the other members of the panel of inquiry. The panel was to be chaired by a barrister, Gerald Kidner, who was assisted by Professor Hunter, an anaesthetist in Manchester, John Constable, the works officer at the West Midlands Regional Health Authority and me, Chairman of NATN. The Inquiry was to start the next morning, 16th March 1976 at the Wolfson School of Nursing. It was to be a private inquiry.

Our terms of reference were 'To inquire into, and determine the cause or causes of the incident affecting Miss Elizabeth Shewan in Operating Theatre B at Westminster Hospital on 21st February 1975' and 'To recommend what steps should be taken to prevent a similar occurrence in the future'. Our report was to go to the Kensington and Chelsea and Westminster Area Health Authority (Teaching) who were responsible for Westminster Hospital.

We gathered in the morning of the 16th March 1976, only to find that Mr. Shewan, the victim's father, had gone to the press and complained that he did not want a private inquiry, but a public one so that lessons would be learnt and be made public. The poor man was distraught with what had happened to his daughter and, as with such cases, he wanted heads to roll.

In view of the publicity in the press the witnesses who were to be interviewed withdrew and refused to give evidence. The inquiry was adjourned but the chairman stated that that would not be the end of the matter.

The Inquiry would have to be provided with the statutory power to compel the attendance of witnesses and it took between March and October that year to set up the Inquiry under Section 70 of the NHS Act 1946. So on the 4th October we started a formal and fully independent inquiry with power to compel the attendance of witnesses under subpoena. Each of the disciplines and firms involved, and there were many, had briefed a QC. Bird & Bird became the solicitors to the inquiry and the venue was moved to the Rembrandt Hotel in London.

Bromley Area Health Authority was asked to release me for a week to take part in the inquiry, but in the event we spent four weeks taking evidence from all disciplines involved as well as staff from the medical firms whose equipment was in use in the theatres. We then had the task of writing the report and making recommendations, of which there were twenty-two. Our report was published in June 1977. It was an interesting but harrowing experience and it taught me a great deal.

The series of incidents that lead to the tragic accident was unbelievable. When I asked the cleaner how he had got his machine caught in the anaesthetic machine that resulted in the hoses becoming detached, he informed me that he had not bothered to move the furniture to clean the floor. A junior nurse on night duty had fixed them back on but had connected the oxygen to the nitrous oxide outlet and the nitrous oxide to the oxygen outlet. The maintenance man from the firm who had the contract to service the anaesthetic machines on a regular basis had not visited the hospital for eighteen months. When I asked him why not, he replied that he could not get a parking space outside the hospital.

There had been other incidents of a similar nature in other hospitals involving anaesthetic gases. The Department of Health had issued hazard notices and technical memoranda to the field units of the NHS concerning these. In the background to our recommendations, we emphasised that in our view the responsibilities of a superior authority are not discharged by the issue of instructions or guidance; that there must be informed knowledge by that authority of the adequacy of available resources of men, money and material to implement those instructions and there must be monitoring to determine whether the objectives are in practice being achieved. The reason for this was that the issued guidance could not be implemented because of a lack of qualified staff and other resources, especially out of hours.

I was to think of this on many occasions when I would find that policies and procedures that had been written by those in authority never ensured that these were not just implemented, but monitored and audited to ensure that they were practical, easy to understand and achievable.

What came out of the inquiry was that anaesthetic hoses became colour-coded so that the same cross-over did not happen again. Hoses were fixed to the anaesthetic machines, compulsory safety checks were introduced and a 'permit to work' system came into being. All of this happened almost forty years ago and now with the increase in sophisticated technology and machinery, there is a clinical engineering department in hospitals and when a new machine is being bought, staff from the department go to the firm for a course in the maintenance of the machine so that they are familiar with its workings. Pre-planned maintenance and warning systems have been introduced along with annual tests.

One of the issues that came to light during the inquiry was that there was no contract for the gas hoses from the wall to the anaesthetic machine. One firm had the contract for the piped gases up to the wall and another firm had the contract for the machines. There was no contract for the hoses in between.

In my own situation, at that time, we had opened new operating theatres with piped gases. I rang the administrator at Bromley Hospital and asked him to meet me later that evening so that we could look at our contracts. The same thing had happened: there was no contract for the hoses from the wall to the machines. It was a case of 'there but for the grace of God go I'.

Safety is of the utmost importance, but when things go wrong we should always remember that no one goes into an operating theatre with the intention of operating on the wrong limb, the wrong side of a patient or leaving swabs or an instrument inside a patient. There is a need to support colleagues at such a time. It is also necessary, of course, to ensure that sloppy practices are not allowed to exist.

Some years later, when I was Chief Nursing Officer in Brighton, I did an audit of the theatres and was pleased to see that the recommendations from our report had been implemented. So often recommendations are not followed, and the same thing happens again, the complex issue of child abuse being a case in point.

It was only recently when I went to look up certain aspects of the Shewan Report that I appreciated the politics and complexity of such inquiries. I went to the National Archives in Kew where there is complete documentation on the inquiry. I found four two-inch thick files with umpteen letters between MPs, medical associations, solicitors, the Westminster Hospital and the Area Health Authority, some demanding a public inquiry on behalf of the family and others protecting their positions. At one stage the poor father had threatened to go on hunger strike. It brought home to me the fact that I was young and pretty inexperienced at the time, but I had learned a great deal that helped me during my career.

SECOND YEAR AS CHAIRMAN

During this year I was involved with the Royal College of Surgeons and the Association of Anaesthetists in drawing up guidance to safeguard against operating on the wrong limb or wrong side of the body as well as drawing up safeguards against leaving swabs and instruments in patients. The NATN also completed a film on aseptic technique as a teaching aid.

I took the film with me went I went to speak at the Nigerian Theatre Nurses' Conference in Lagos in February 1977. If my visit to South Africa had been a cultural shock, it was nothing compared to this visit to Nigeria. It was a very poor country at that time, as oil had not yet been discovered there.

I was put up in the University campus where the Conference and exhibition were to be held. I was given a very young Nigerian boy to look after me. It was steaming hot, there was no air conditioning and the mosquito net over my bed was full of holes, so I arrived at the Conference with bites all over my face.

The Conference was due to start at 9am and the Minister for Health was coming to open the exhibition. In the event, he never arrived as he had been dismissed from his post. It was rumoured that he had disciplined an orthopaedic surgeon who had been amputating limbs and he had applied plaster casts too tightly, causing gangrene. Those in overall power were of the same tribe as the orthopaedic surgeon, whereas the Minister of Health was from a different tribe, so it was agreed to give him the chop. There was a further rumour that the Minister had returned to the police force from which he had come and this was interpreted as a term in prison.

The chief nursing officer eventually opened the Conference at 11am. I gave my opening address and presented the Chairman of the Association with a gavel. The country may have been poor but the people were welcoming and interesting. The conditions in which they worked were appalling due to the hot weather, the lack of electricity and the frequency of cuts. The new University Hospital in Lagos was being built and I was taken round the far from completed building. I was amazed to see monitors already on the walls of the theatres and intensive care units, as the walls had not yet been plastered. I visited a hospital in Ibadan and had some interesting discussions with the nurses who wanted to know what was news in UK nursing.

On the final night of the Conference there was a dinner in one of the hotels. Just as the dinner was finishing, I was approached and asked to give the vote of thanks. I stuck to thanking everyone for inviting me and mentioned the need for good relationships between their health service and the exhibitors who were the suppliers of goods and equipment. I still have pictures of myself speaking with sweat pouring down my face because of the failure of the air conditioning.

At the dinner, I noticed a small group of women sitting together who looked sad and depressed. I learned that they were English nurses who had married Nigerian doctors when the doctors were undertaking training in the UK. These women had returned with their Nigerian husbands and had had children. The husbands then took other wives as that was the custom, but the English wives did not expect that to happen to them. The wives decided to go back to the UK. Their husbands told them that they could return, but that their children would remain in Nigeria. They were trapped, hence the sad, hopeless faces.

At the end of the dinner after midnight, the managing Director for Johnson & Johnson, Nigeria, told me that he had to go to the telecommunication centre to ring his boss in America. As I had not spoken to Leslie for two weeks because of the non-availability of telephones, I asked to go with him and try and get through. So we went in full evening dress to the centre and booked our calls. Three minutes to England cost £27, a lot of money in 1977. At about 2am, we were called to booths and I was put through. It was wonderful to speak to Leslie and I looked forward to seeing him a few days later.

One evening, driving home late with the President of the Nigerian Nurses' Association, soldiers brandishing guns stopped us and ordered us out of the car. They searched the car and then let us proceed. We asked them what was going on and they replied that we would soon find out. Following this episode, I was quite pleased to get on the plane home. Unfortunately, these are my main memories of my visit to Nigeria, but it must be remembered that the country had come out of a bloody and destructive civil war in 1970, seven years earlier. This war was known as the Biafran War as well as the Nigerian Civil War.

During my first year I became concerned about the business arrangements of the Association. Whether I had acquired business acumen from my father or not, I was concerned that we seem to have all our eggs in one basket, i.e. the same firm did all our printing and ran our exhibition. We even had our meetings in the firm's building in Matlock in Derbyshire.

After Michael Vickers became our new President in October 1976 I had a meeting with him and we discussed where the Association was heading. He asked me what I wanted to achieve during my term as chairman and I expressed the wish that, as well as increasing the membership and getting more educational programmes going, I wanted to put the Association on a more secure financial footing. I knew that by cutting out the middleman our exhibition would be a source of good income. I had also being approached by exhibitors who felt the same as I did.

We decided to go for it but we needed to get the agreement of the executive. Many were apprehensive about such a move, but we agreed in January 1977 that the matter be investigated further and discussed at branch level. I had, with others, attended an exhibition in London organised by the Association of Anaesthetists who had produced a guidance document on how to organise a trade exhibition. At the next executive meeting in July 1977 I spelled out areas where money was needed, such as further education, study days, films, recruitment, public relations and the general running of the Association.

Agreement was reached to manage our own exhibition in 1978, with all profits coming to NATN, in spite of opposition from some quarters. Michael agreed to be adviser to the working group to bring it about. The exhibitors formed an exhibitors' committee and there was close working with them, which was a great help in the success of this venture. The exhibition went from strength to strength. We had 87 stands in our first year, 1978, and this had increased to 180, the best ever, eight years later.

The theme for the 13th Conference in Harrogate was 'Broader Horizons' and I felt that the Association was beginning to look to broader horizons at that time. After much discussion and a lot of hard work by the Yorkshire Branch, we opened our first headquarters in Harrogate at 22 Mount Parade, a cause for much celebration. We had our meetings there from then on, having vacated the office in Matlock and transferred our equipment to the new headquarters.

We shared with the executive our plans for the 14th Conference and exhibition that would be held in Brighton. It was another risk that we were taking as Harrogate had been the conference centre for years and it meant that members from the north of England and Scotland would have further to travel. Moreover, it was a new centre which constituted another risk. However, there had been pressure from southern branches to have the conference in the south and it was also felt that while we remained in

Harrogate, prices would continue to increase as the town council thought we would continue to go there.

During the year I reported on progress on the Health Notice HC(76)38 'Pollution of operating theatres, etc. by anaesthetic gases'. The working party on which we were represented had met and research was ongoing on establishing the level of pollution and the change that scavenging devices would bring about.

We were active in the field of education, especially continuing education, and an initial meeting was held with the Joint Board of Clinical Nursing Studies, the body responsible for post-basic education. We agreed that a day release course would be possible and meetings followed to bring this about. Part-time courses for theatre nurses were discussed. This would be feasible and would last over a period of two years instead of the one-year for full-time courses.

The staffing and training subcommittee drew up a completed code of practice and this was made available to members at the Conference. As well as the official programme, informal sessions were held for the first time at the 1977 Conference on 'Pollution of operating theatres', 'Pre-and post-operative visiting' and 'Staffing Levels', topics that were of great relevance at the time.

THIRD AND FINAL YEAR AS CHAIRMAN

At the Council meeting in January, I announced that I had been invited to speak at both the opening and at an educational session at the Association of Operating Room Nurses' Congress in New Orleans in March 1978. It was their Silver anniversary Congress and it was agreed that I should go.

The AORN Congress was a great success; the lectures were interesting and informative and the social events were wonderful. One of my lasting memories is of the dinner when the sweet was being served. It was baked Alaska and it was carried in, flaming, by ten black waiters to the tune of 'When the Saints go marching in' with the room in complete darkness. There were about three thousand theatre nurses at the Congress, which included twelve members of NATN.

In my opening address, I congratulated AORN and thanked them for their assistance to NATN over the years and to me personally when I was undertaking my scholarship. I spoke of our special relationship and the need to continue to work together for the benefit of patient care.

My address in the educational session was entitled 'Theatre nurses meet changing social needs'. On reading it now, it was really informing the audience about what was happening in Britain in the changing health scene and the role that nurses were playing in this scenario. I stressed the expansion of primary care services that had become the Government's top priority. The expansion meant looking after more people in the community to help relieve pressure on hospital services. That was 35 years ago and one can question if in fact we have moved far and fast enough in this expansion. More importantly, have the resources shifted to meet it or have the acute services continued to eat up the resources as techniques and interventions continue to increase as technology develops at such a rate?

In referring to the changes in nurse education and the proposals in the Briggs Report, it was not clear if student nurses would get sufficient experience in theatre work to give them a full picture on the care of the surgical patient. I questioned the effect this would have on theatre staffing.

Our entry into the European Economic Community had also affected nursing. Directives had been formulated to ensure common training so that qualified nurses could work in the eight member states at that time — Britain, France, West Germany, Holland, Italy, Belgium, Ireland and Luxembourg.

I mentioned that there were at the time 46 post-graduate courses throughout Britain to accommodate nurses who wished to specialize in theatre nursing. This was the largest number of any of the special post-basic courses offered by the Joint Board of Clinical Nursing Studies. I explained that a short course for experienced theatre nurses would be set up to accommodate NATN's objective of continuing education.

I informed them about what was happening with our operating department assistants, their courses and their role vis-à-vis theatre nursing staff. Importantly the Department of Health report on the promotion of this new grade stated that the nurse is in charge of the operating department at all times and that the new grade is responsible to the nurse as the person qualified in all aspects of patient care. Operating department staff had opened their doors to increase communication with the wards and with other departments by participation in ward rounds and by pre-operative and post-operative visits. This had resulted in an improvement in both the physical and psychological care of the surgical patient.

My talk was well received and it was printed in total in the AORN Journal in September 1978. I enjoyed New Orleans, a beautiful city, and it was with a heavy heart that I watched on television the damage done by the flooding when the storms smashed the levees some years ago.

I spent some nervous times on the run-up to our 1978 Congress because of the risks we were taking in organising our own exhibition. There were trips to Brighton to check on the facilities during the summer. The Grand Hotel was to be the Congress hotel, now famous for the devastating bombing during the Conservative Party Conference in 1984, weeks after I had become chief nursing officer for Brighton Area Health Authority.

By the time of the Congress in November industrial action affecting the health service had already started. The winter of 1978/79 was to become known as 'The Winter of Discontent'. Although the Labour Government of the day had promised a return to collective bargaining, wage restraint was to continue, much to the annoyance and frustration of trade union members who resorted to strike action.

The theme of my last Congress was 'Back to Basics' and my keynote speech contained raillery against the cutbacks and the petty changes that were taking place. It had become necessary to fill in a form to get a sandwich in the middle of the night while on an emergency call-out, and having to pay another 2p for a dollop of salad cream on the rare occasion when you got a chance to go for a meal in the dining room. These and other changes were sapping morale and putting another nail in the coffin of the NHS. I voiced concern that the professional voice was not being listened to and this was causing the goodwill of staff to wane and be replaced with frustration. I stressed the need for an improvement in industrial relations; otherwise patients would be put in danger.

There were those in the audience who, like me, had driven through picket lines to get into the hospital if there was an emergency or urgent case that had to be operated on. As well as our theatre duties, we had to go to the ward to get the patient, do all the lifting and then return the patient to the ward as all portering staff were on strike.

It was also a time when nurses were being encouraged to extend their role, in spite of the fact that there was a staff shortage. I used the 'Back to Basics' theme to caution that as patient stay was decreasing rapidly, we needed to remember that our role is to nurse sick people and that instead of going on a crash course on intravenous technique and intubation, we should take ourselves off on a course on the psychology of communications and the effects of isolation and fear.

At the Annual General Meeting at the end of Congress, I was expecting a lot of complaints from the northerners on the distance to travel and from all on the more expensive venue. But there were none and I put that down to the fact that the sun had shone for the whole time and the temperature was in the 70s, with people walking on the promenade in short sleeves. At the Annual General Meeting, I passed over to the vice-chairman, Mollie Whittaker, and thus ended three jam-packed great years of my career.

BACK TO BROMLEY

I returned to the theatres full time and thanked my staff and my employing authority for all the support that they had given me. Although I loved running operating theatres, I felt it was time to move on. I had been advised to do so by my seniors and the following year an opportunity arose that I had to consider. The matron of Bromley Hospital had decided to retire and the post was advertised. I decided that the benefits of being promoted in the hospital with which I was familiar outweighed the disadvantage of being in a position of authority over those who had been colleagues.

The Salmon Report, which was introduced following its acceptance in 1966, brought in a structure of management for nursing, part of which was the introduction of new titles. I had been 'converted' from being theatre superintendent to nursing officer theatres when the Salmon Report was implemented, although the medical staff continued to call me 'sister'. That was their way of showing their disapproval for the whole report and its implementation. I had changed my title and place in the structure, but my role remained unchanged as I was a hands-on person and remained part of the theatre team.

The structure brought about more layers of management that were supposed to help those who had the appropriate skills through experience and training to take more senior positions and be capable of undertaking the roles. As usual, when it came to financing training, there was no money as a result of the sterling crisis of 1966. It was a case of accepting the report, but there was no money to implement it as intended. The nursing officer post for wards, for example those for surgical and for medicine, were often filled by assistant matrons who had been away from the clinical areas for many years, were out of date and were seen as a threat to the ward sisters. In my own situation, apart from me and the nursing officer for the Accident and Emergency Department and Intensive Care Unit, these were viewed as administration posts that further increased the criticism from medical staff and were a disincentive for senior sisters wishing to advance. It was to be many years before what was intended, and indeed needed, was introduced in the setting up of clinical nurse practitioners and consultant nurses.

One factor that I recognised from the Salmon Report was the need to undergo further training in management and I applied and was accepted for the Diploma in Management Studies run by Woolwich Polytechnic. This was run on a day-release over two years. It proved an interesting course and I learned a lot about health economics. It brought home to me the dilemma for nurses regarding what has been referred to as the 'cash and care dilemma'. Professional staff always want to do the best for patients, and rightly so, but do not want to accept that resources are not finite and choices have to be made. There is not a bottomless pit of money and professionals appear at times not to recognise this fact. They are reluctant to bring about change that is necessary as tribal warfare and a possible change in power base prevents this happening.

The post of matron was advertised as 'senior nursing officer' (SNO) and I became one in 1979, following a selection process. The folly of changing the title was brought home to me early on by the patients when I went on ward rounds. I would introduce my self as the SNO for the hospital and blank faces were the result. Once I said I was the matron, everyone relaxed and they would chat to me about their care, progress, the food and the caring staff.

I always undertook ward rounds unannounced as I felt that this was the way to get the feel of the ambiance on the wards and departments and find out whether the care was satisfactory. On other occasions I went with the domestic supervisor unannounced to ensure that the standards of cleanliness and hygiene were good. I am, of course relating to a time when the misuse and abuse of antibiotics had not started and the super bugs had not arrived on the horizon. The nutrition of patients was the responsibility of the ward sister and her team.

I settled into the role and enjoyed it with its many ups and downs. One of the downs was that I was trying to run a hospital that had an A & E department without enough supporting beds for admissions. I discovered that patients were being moved to a nearby hospital at all hours of the day and night when emergency admissions could not be found beds and were too ill to be moved themselves.

At that time we had a tripartite system of managing the hospital made up of a consultant, an administrator and me. We discussed the distress the situation was causing patients and their relatives and took the following course of action. As most emergency admissions occurred at the weekend, it was decided that I would do a ward round with the appropriate medical registrar on the Friday and move patients then while there was still time to inform relatives and plan the moves carefully. This eased the situation while we waited for the ward block that was never built. It was the first of many examples that I was to encounter of a lack of long-term forward planning in the health service.

I have always been wary of nurses extending their role without the necessary resources of staff and training. There is always a danger that basic care will be ignored while nurses take on roles that are seen as more prodigious and give them enhanced status. One day a very angry gentleman barged through my office door and demanded that I explain why the A&E nurses were not caring for his elderly mother who was waiting on a trolley without anyone seeing to her. He was a general practitioner in the area and was appalled at the lack of care being received by his mother. I apologized and accompanied him to the department and sorted things out. But that was not the end of it. I was angry and unhappy that this woman did not receive good care in 'my' hospital.

The apartment was well staffed and I called the sisters together at lunchtime and asked them what was going on. After some shifting and shuffling, they admitted that they were supervising the house officers who did not know what they were doing most of the time. I asked what the consultant for the department was doing as it was the job of the consultant to supervise. Again, there was some shifting and shuffling and then it came out that the consultant was rarely in the department; they alleged that an affair was taking place with one of the ambulance crew. I brought the matter to the attention of the consultant on our management team and things were sorted out. I did not receive any more complaints after that, but I remained wary of the extended role for nurses.

One day I returned from a meeting to find one of the sisters in the foyer of the hospital crying her eyes out. She had been off sick and I took her to my office to find out what was upsetting her. Janet had been a colleague for many years, she was a good nurse and I was very fond of her. She had been to see one of the consultants who had informed her that he thought that she was alcoholic and he wanted her to go to the alcoholic clinic at King's College Hospital. She had refused to go, denying that she was alcoholic. I tried to persuade her that she should go but she only agreed when I promised that I would go with her.

The day of the appointment arrived and while at the clinic I sat in the waiting room while she was seen, and wondered if any of the people milling about knew me and wondered what I was doing there. The doctor then saw me, with her permission, and advised me that she had a problem and I would need to assess her future employment. With her agreement I moved her to out-patients where she would not be handling drugs, had regular meetings with her and there were no further problems while I was in post.

The consultant who diagnosed Janet's illness was also a senior consultant at King's College Hospital, a large teaching hospital in London. His name was John Dawson and there is now a ward called the John Dawson Ward at King's. He was a great surgeon and his untimely death from hepatitis, caught from a patient, was a terrible loss to medicine and to me as he had became a friend as well as a colleague.

Medicine and surgery, at that time, were advancing rapidly and very often the teaching hospitals were involved in complicated work rather than the 'bread and butter' stuff such as hernias and varicose veins. John was worried that the medical students were missing out on the basics and asked me if some of the junior medical students could come to Bromley Hospital to gain experience. I agreed and plans were made to accommodate them. When they started I went to meet them with John and he warned them that they were to do what 'sis' said and behave. He was a disciplinarian and one day a student appeared in a polo neck sweater under his white coat. John glared at him and told him to go the change into a collar and tie out of respect for the patients who were giving him the privilege of learning from them. How the world has changed.

MORE REORGANISATION

The structure brought in by the Salmon Report was the first of many reorganisations that were to influence my career in the years ahead. New management arrangements outlined in what became known as the 'Grey Book' were introduced in 1974. A Royal Commission Report on the NHS was published in 1979. In 1982, as a result of the reorganisation of nursing services, I left Bromley Hospital in what were, looking back, rather bizarre circumstances. Director of Nursing Posts replaced Senior Nursing Officers. We had to apply for five posts at the same level and the five hospitals applied to had to say after interview whom they wanted, who was their first choice then their second and so on. Following our five interviews, we had to give our first choice, then our second and so on. The five had to be in the region in which the applicant worked. Mine was the South East Thames Region. We were then matched up, rather like football teams are picked to play each other in the top football leagues.

I played safe by applying for my own post. The other four were Maidstone, Brighton, King's College and Lewisham/Hither Green which formed one unit. I drove around the region to the interviews. I even had two on the one day, one at King's and one for Lewisham/Hither Green. The second one was at Guy's and when someone asked the same question that I had been asked at King's, I got totally confused and told the panel I had already answered that. Whoever dreamed up this process of selection should have been shot. There was not only the financial cost but also the destabilising and demoralising effect on staff at all levels.

I put my first choice as Lewisham/Hither Green, an area of great diversity where there were black and ethnic groups in the population and in the staff. It had previously been a Health Authority in its own right but was now the poorer end of what became Lewisham and North Southwark Area Health Authority, following an amalgamation with Guy's Health Authority. I decided that my choice would be the most challenging and so it turned out to be. We were definitely the poor relation to the posh Guy's Teaching Hospital, and so had received limited resources over the years compared with Guy's who benefited from many large donations from benefactors.

All of these re-organisations had a devastating effect on staff at all levels, but especially those in senior positions. Politicians would appear to give no thought to the upheaval caused. In their efforts to reform the House of Lords we have seen attempts made to do so but the status quo remains. Yet those of us in the health service have to go along with politicians' wishes, some not thought through. Over the years the health service remains a political football.

It was no wonder then, with senior staff not knowing what their jobs would be in the future, that eyes were taken off the ball in the managing of staff, making decisions and ensuring that patient care was of good quality. So I should not have been surprised to find that in my new post there was much to do. My primary objective was and always had been, to ensure that patient care was safe, that staff treated patients with dignity and respect and that nursing practice was of a high standard.

I had concerns about an elderly care ward at Hither Green Hospital, but could not put my finger on it when I was doing a ward round with the charge nurse. The patients were men who would discuss with me their past lives and the horseracing, if it was on the television. I still introduced myself as the matron so that they would know who I was. The story is told of the Queen Mother who when visiting an elderly care ward asked a patient if he knew who she was. The reply that she got was 'Go and see the ward sister and she will sort you out'.

I decided to call in on the ward on my way home one evening. I found all the nurses in the ward office ticking off the menu cards for the next day. I confronted the charge nurse and was told that the men were incapable of making a choice. I did not accept this and suggested that we go and talk to the patients. At the same time I looked round the ward and noted that one patient was missing. We went to the toilet area and I found the man tied to a chair in the bathroom. I suspended the charge nurse and following a hearing he was sacked. He appealed and there was a hearing by non-executive members of the Health Authority. My action was upheld.

In preparing myself for the hearing I had spoken to the consultant for the ward. I asked him if he had concerns about the patients in his care. He replied that he had, but that he played badminton with the charge nurse and did not like to complain.

Unfortunately this was not the only dismissal that I had to deal with during my time in post. One of the nursing officers had been off on long-term sickness. Then I found out that he was working in a café. That, of course, was totally unacceptable. Some of his staff had seen him there, making matters worse. I asked to see him and he came accompanied with his union representative. I learned that he was suffering from a mental illness, so it was suggested that he should retire on health grounds. His representative agreed with me but he did not. He was in a position in charge of other staff and could be involved in the administration of drugs, as well as making decisions on patient care. Although we pleaded with him he refused to retire and I had no option but to dismiss him. He dumped his sensible union representative, joined another union and took me to an industrial tribunal for unfair dismissal.

The Director of Human Resources who was to accompany me and state my case was new in post so I found myself in the farcical situation of stating my case and then going into the witness box to give evidence to the members of the panel, who then questioned me. The Chairman, who must always be a lawyer, did not have a clue about the Health Service and after many hours of questioning, made a request that I find a job for him consisting of menial tasks, but that I keep him on a nursing officer's salary. I explained that this was impossible and that my concern was patient safety. I won the case, but never wanted to go through that again.

There were other disciplinary actions I had to take and it was then that I realised the dilemma facing the Royal College of Nursing (RCN) which is our professional body but also a trade union. I am a member of the RCN and so would expect support when needing to address professional issues. However, I have been through cases when an RCN representative has been representing and supporting nurses who have behaved badly to patients and put patients at risk, such as the giving of wrong drugs.

Combining the role of professional body and trade union in 1977 was, in my view, a mistake and the profession has missed out on not having a body totally dedicated to standards and development of nursing practice. The medical profession has been more sensible keeping Royal Colleges for professional issues while the British Medical Association manages pay, negotiations and support for its members. Recently, the Francis Report into poor care made a recommendation that the RCN needed to review its role both as a professional body and a trade union.

I had found previously that if you do not monitor sickness levels, they will get out of control, with agency nurses being employed to fill the gap leading to overspend on budgets. There is the occupational health department to ensure genuine sickness is dealt with sensitively. Each Regional Health Authority produced a print-out of sickness for each hospital/unit. I decided to have a look at these, highlighting anyone who had over twelve days' sickness in the year. This did not include those who I knew were on long-term sickness. To my horror, I found out that I was highlighting most of the staff. I gave the print-outs to the senior nurses for each unit and asked them to investigate.

The result was a queue waiting to be interviewed in the occupational health department, some weeks after I had done my investigation. We had many black and ethnic groups on the staff so it was not surprising that there were many in the queue from these backgrounds. The occupational doctor had a wobbly and rang me to say that I would be reported to the Race Relations Board.

This did not happen, but I became aware that weak managers used the Race Relations Act to avoid taking action when the offence or need for discipline did not have anything to do with the colour of the person's skin. I also discovered that in the Intensive Therapy Unit (ITU) when agency nurses were being employed they always came from the same agency, which also had on their books many of the ITU staff who wanted to do extra hours. I thought that this could be open to abuse and asked to see the nurse in charge. He resigned immediately without speaking to me and it was the only time in my life that I got a threatening phone call that was anonymous. The caller advised me that I should watch it as my car might be dangerous to drive. I can only assume that the call came from the agency we no longer used.

One day three student nurses came to see me as they were concerned about aspects of care on one of the wards on which they had worked. They had reported it but nothing had happened. Through unannounced visits and meetings with the ward sister and the manager for the area, I discovered that there was an uncaring culture on the ward but nobody did anything. Disciplinary action was taken and things improved. We have had many scandals in the health service recently, the mid-Staffordshire Trust being one. Although problems were reported on many occasions, no action was taken, with disastrous consequences. I firmly believe that if there is any whiff that something is wrong and the matter is brought up with senior staff and nothing happens, then the senior staff are as guilty, if not more so, of the offence. When these offences are against vulnerable people, it is a disgrace. Evil continues if good men (and women) remain silent.

There have always been barrels that contain bad apples. If not removed, then the whole barrel can be affected and bring about poor patient care. To continue with this metaphor, if the keeper or keepers of the barrel do nothing about the bad apples due to lack of monitoring and inspection, then they are to blame for putting patients at risk of poor care and attention. The keepers of units in the health service start with the executives and non-executives of the board and run down through the lines of accountability. When no one is held to account, the destructive media from whom the health service continues to suffer, have a field day and the public begins to lose faith in the health service.

When I left the comfort zone of the operating theatres, I was conceited enough to think that by rising up the ranks, I could influence more in a larger arena. To deny the fact that an increase in salary would be welcomed would be a lie. My time in Lewisham/Hither Green taught me a great deal about industrial relations and the power struggles between professionals that were very often about personalities rather than patients. The medical profession was, and always will be, the most powerful group and no one wanted to upset them. It was difficult to engage them in improvements in patient care. At times I thought that their agenda was more about getting sessions at Guy's that would enhance their curriculum vitae thus increasing their private practice.

A great deal of money was spent doing an option appraisal on deciding where the new headquarters of the reformed Lewisham and North Southwark Area Health Authority, which was the joining of Lewisham/Hither Green with Guy's Hospital, would be.

We were all aware that it would be Guy's but it had to be seen that the matter had been fully negotiated with staff groups. The result of Guy's as the best option meant that I spent many hours travelling between Lewisham and Guy's, where all meetings were held.

My big ambition at this time was to become a chief nursing officer (CNO) to an Area Health Authority. As it was only five years, at that time, since I had left operating theatres, I thought it would be worthwhile to apply to see if I would be short-listed and, if I was lucky enough to get an interview, to know what kind of questions I might be asked and find out what further reading/preparation I would need to undertake so that I would eventually get a CNO post. The post of CNO came up at Brighton Health Authority so I decided to go for it with no expectation of being selected and was surprised that I was short-listed. The post involved being in overall charge of nursing in each of the units, of which where were five, and the School of Nursing. The units were the Royal Sussex Hospital and Sussex Eye Hospital which dealt with acute work, the Brighton General which dealt with elderly care and where the headquarters of the Area Health Authority were based. There was a unit dealing with mental health, one for those with learning difficulties and one for community services. Each had a Director of Nursing included in the Management Team and the School of Nursing also had a Director.

My expectation was further lowered at the 'Trial by Sherry' which was the reception before the formal interviews, where the members of the board and the management team were given the opportunity to meet the candidates. It was a bit crowded. I had a glass of red wine in my hand. Someone brushed past me and the glass of wine went right down the trousers of the member of the board with whom I was having a serious conversation. The board member let out a high-pitched squeal, the room became silent and all turned towards us. My embarrassment knew no bounds.

This must have relaxed me for the formal interview, believing I did not stand a chance so I was amazed the next day to have a phone call from the Chairman, Julia Cumberlege (now Baroness Cumberlege), offering me the job. It meant moving house but Leslie, a design consultant with his studio in Newcastle, had his own business with clients around the country, many in Scotland, so it did not matter to him where we lived.

BRIGHTON HEALTH AUTHORITY

We moved to the Brighton area in September 1984, just three weeks before the Brighton bombing in the Grand Hotel. I got a call in the middle of the night and went to the Royal Sussex Hospital where the casualties were being taken. The director of nursing for the hospital, Eileen Brennan, was already there, as well as other members of the management team. I was new in post and unfamiliar with the hospital so I asked Eileen where I could best help. I shadowed her and went on messages to various departments and helped out where I could.

It was a surreal situation because those injured were high profile politicians. There was a large media presence, both television and press, and we set up an office for them in the casualty department. We did not wish them to move from there but we brought them news as events unfolded. I kept thinking 'I know you' and then realising it was one of the faces seen daily on television news. There was also a large police presence.

As the morning wore on, the pressmen became restive so we decided to escort them to talk to some of the wounded who were happy and well enough to be interviewed. The press officer led the way and I was following at the rear of the group. We were aware that the real story would be to interview Norman Tebbitt, whose wife had been seriously injured in the blast. Before long one of the group decided to leave it and I stepped in to stop him. He began to become abusive to me and immediately a plain clothes policeman appeared and instructed him to join the main group or he would be thrown out of the hospital. The policeman continued to follow the group out of sight. If I was ever threatened he would suddenly pop out from somewhere to support me. He said to me 'We have got to stop meeting like this'. Even horrendous situations have their light moments.

My other vivid recollection of that day was when John Wakeham was brought into the Accident and Emergency department. It was lunchtime and he had been in the rubble of the Grand Hotel from about three o'clock in the morning when the bomb went off.

He was a blue-green colour and in pain. The consultant in charge was Tony Trafford who had been a politician with Margaret Thatcher. He became the main contact with her in the following weeks and became Lord Trafford some years later. Tony rang Northern Ireland, where the experts on crush injuries were working at the time, as a result of the Troubles. They advised him not to operate and gave him instructions as to the appropriate care. Many months later John Wakeham entered the House of Commons on two sticks to the cheers of all sides of the House. So out of all the evil at that time came some good.

The nurse in charge of the Intensive Care Unit was Irish and he told me later that he said to John Wakeham that it was ironic that he had to put up with an Irishman looking after him. John Wakeham's reply was that there was good and evil in all nationalities. Mrs Tebbitt was also in the Intensive Care Unit but before long it became obvious that she needed the facilities available at Stoke Mandeville Hospital. This needed some organisation, as it had to be done without interference from the media personnel who maintained a vigil outside the main entrance to the Accident and Emergency department. With the combined services of the RAF and Ambulance Service, Mrs Tebbit was taken out the back of the hospital to a waiting helicopter in an adjacent playing field before anyone knew what was going on.

When thinking back to those horrendous events in Brighton, it is great to know that the nurses were excellent in caring for the wounded and those who had lost close and loved ones at the time. A recent book entitled 'Nurses' Voices' tells of the events recalled by the nurses in Northern Ireland and what they went through during those terrible times. It reminded me of those surreal days in Brighton that were luckily a one off.

Once things died down and the media and politicians were no longer part of our life, I nominated Eileen Brennan for an honour as she had done a great job in organising resources to deal with a major incident. She was duly awarded the Order of the British Empire (OBE).

Griffiths Report

The year of the Brighton bombing, 1984, was also the year when a bombshell hit the health service, in particular the nursing profession. The year before, Roy Griffiths, the managing director of Sainsbury's, had been commissioned to advise the Secretary of State for Health on the effective use and management of manpower and related resources in the NHS. He and three other people, a personnel director from British Telecom, a financial director from United Biscuits and a regional administrator, had produced the recommendations, which became known as the Griffiths Report.

The main recommendations brought about general management, with an all-powerful general manager at all levels, Regional and Area

Health Authorities and units. It did away with functional management and consensus management resulting in the demise of professional power in the NHS, especially among nurses.

The first sign that senior nurses were seen as unimportant was when the supervisory board that was to be chaired by the Secretary of State was set up. The board was to consist of the permanent secretary, the chief medical officer, the chairman of the management board and two or three non-executive members. The chief nursing officer was not included.

The appointment of general managers then occurred rapidly, and Brighton Health Authority (BHA) appointed their administrator, David Bowden, as their general manager. This happened with many administrators. Each year BHA held an event at which staff from all the disciplines were recognised and rewarded for being outstanding members of staff.

This event occurred just after David was appointed and it was agreed that the chief executive on the supervisory board, Duncan Nichol, be invited to officiate. David was a great one for practical jokes and I decided to play one on him. That morning we met in David's office to check arrangements for the day. Before we started I informed David that none of the nurses would be attending as we wanted to show Duncan Nichol that we were upset that the chief nursing officer had been slighted in this way. Poor David was livid and the personnel director who was responsible for the arrangements went pale.

I was amazed that they believed that I could influence all the nurses, who numbered about 2,000 and many of whom were to receive awards, to take such action. I could not keep a straight face and burst out laughing. David promised to get me for it and of course he did on many occasions. He would frequently remind me that the red wine stain on 'his' carpet was my doing.

The nursing profession was most affected as nurses were no longer in charge of nurses but became responsible to general managers who knew little about nursing and the role of nurses. My role was now called chief nursing advisor although I continued to call myself chief nursing officer. The management role along with the nursing budget went from me and from the director of nursing in each of the units to the appropriate general manager.

My role was now to advise on nursing matters, and that advice could be taken or not, so the role became a very frustrating one. Advice is only pleasant for those giving it and it is not very often well received by those who ask for it. At times, I regrettably took out my frustration on some staff who were possibly unaware of how much I resented what was happening to my profession.

Roy Griffiths had given the assurance that 'nurses would still lead nursing', but that is not the same as leading nurses in the importance of safe and high quality patient care. Consensus management always frustrated administrators, many of who had become general managers and who resented the fact that nurses and doctors could hinder what they wanted to do. At times it seemed that old scores were being settled.

It was a sad time for chief nursing officers as their powers, influence and span of control were dramatically reduced. At each meeting we had with the Regional Nursing Officer, we said goodbye to one of our colleagues who was not prepared to put up with the new arrangements. The nursing expertise lost to the health service was a disaster as we became increasingly marginalised and excluded from the policy-making function at all levels.

In 1987 I was invited to give the Daisy Ayris Memorial lecture at the NATN Conference in Harrogate, a place that will always have fond memories for me. I used the occasion to try and spell out how the nursing profession allowed itself to be beheaded while we slept soundly in our beds. I entitled my talk 'Educate that you may be free'. That was what an Irish revolutionary had advised an oppressed people to do many years ago. I stressed that we needed to be free from the image of the nurse in the eyes of the public and other disciplines. One image is of the sex symbol, the dumb blonde in black stockings who flirts with the doctor as per the Mills and Boon novel. Another is the image of the nurse as the administering angel. These images ensure that the nurse is seen not as a skilled practitioner, carrying out a difficult and complex role, but as the handmaiden of the doctor whose slightest whinge is her command.

There had been many reports on the need to change and improve nurse education at all levels but we had failed to get action as we fought among ourselves. Others used this to prevent progress in nurse education, which was badly needed. It was as if we were still back in the days of Florence Nightingale. When she was trying to establish a training school at St Thomas' Hospital, a surgeon, John Flint South, let it be known that he considered nurses needed no more qualifications than housemaids.

Would better educated nurses have been able to state their case in ensuring that our power base was not swept away from under our feet? Would such nurses have educated the public on our changing role and our importance in achieving quality of care? As the most numerous discipline in the health service, we needed to learn to stick together and have a united voice. We needed nurse leaders who did not rely on the image of the administering angel to cover up our inadequacies in stating our case. We needed leaders who were educated in health economics and negotiating skills, and able to put forward sound examples to improve patient care that did not always cost money. This knowledge might have prevented the catastrophe that the nursing profession endured. I am afraid that I allowed my bitterness to show, but it was obvious that many in the audience felt the same as I did. It was the only time that I ever got a standing ovation.

The RCN woke up too late to do anything to reverse the situation although it did manage, following extensive lobbying, to get the chief nursing officer reinstated on the supervisory board. It was alleged that the RCN was hoping to get an increase in salaries for its members so had dragged its feet on the Griffiths Report with a disastrous result for the profession. Once again, it showed up the understandable conflict when an organisation is both the professional body and the trade union.

As well as devastating nursing roles and structures, the new agenda was to get value for money. Comparisons were made between high- and low-spending authorities with the result that quality of care was challenged and, in some circumstances, compromised in the name of saving more and more money and resources. At the same time, quality assurance was to balance the relentless quest for more savings. 'Achieve more with less' is also the motto today in health care and everywhere else.

CONSUMER AFFAIRS

It would be foolish to say that everything in the garden was rosy before the Griffiths Report. As my role was diminished through losing the budget and management of nurses, I was given the role of director of consumer affairs. This involved monitoring the services through the eyes of those receiving them, and a very enlightening experience it proved. There is arrogance among those of us running the health services and giving the care that we know what is right for patients, but this is not always the case. Having services free at the point of delivery contributes to the attitude of 'take it or leave it' and it is often forgotten that we are paying for the health service through our taxes.

On a trip to outpatients, I encountered a sister with arms folded in an aggressive stance, advising a patient that he was lucky that he had only waited for an hour and that patients had waited two hours the day before. I decided to do something about waits in outpatients and spoke to the consultants about altering their booking-in systems. I had full support from the chairman and David. This was just as well as there was open hostility towards what I was trying to do to help reduce the long waits that patients were undergoing. The consultants advised me that they would have to wait for patients in between consultations if the bookings were altered to a target waiting time of thirty minutes and that there would be no way that they could see as many patients during a session. I assured them that we would ensure that they would see the same number but without the long waits and they would not be kept waiting. One consultant informed me that if he opened the consulting room door and there were not many people waiting, he would not work so fast. I threatened to get dummies and put them in the waiting area,

Another outpatient department of concern was for those with appointments to see the eye consultants. The waiting time for new patients was six months, unacceptable for such a vital organ. On investigation, I found that people whose eyesight had deteriorated to the point that nothing else could be done for them were still coming back to the clinic, thus blocking new referrals. When I asked the consultants why, I was informed that they did not like telling people that their eyesight could not be improved. I felt this was wrong and these people would benefit from the services of the associations for the blind.

The worst clinics were the phlebotomy ones as there was no booking-in system. Everyone arrived at the same time and then had to have blood taken, get the result, see a doctor and get their prescription changed and then queue again for the pharmacy. I spoke to the patients. Some came from a distance, some by ambulance, as the service was concentrated in one area in Brighton. The patients told me that they would be ready at seven in the morning so as not to keep the ambulance waiting. Some came early and queued outside the department so as to be first in the queue. Having spoken to the patients and the relatives, the end result was that we arranged for this service to be delivered in health centres nearer to the population.

Other services I reviewed were those involved in the treatment of cancer patients, i.e. radiotherapy and chemotherapy. I found that the radiotherapy department only operated between nine in the morning and midday and then from two to five in the afternoon. I was at a loss to understand why very expensive machinery was lying idle for so much of the day. I then found out that the staff played bridge at lunchtime for two hours. The services were rearranged from eight in the morning till six in the evening and the bridge had to stop as the department stayed open over lunchtime. The morning and evening extended sessions allowed those in employment not to be away from their place of work for longer than was necessary.

Chemotherapy had not been developed to today's standard and many patients to whom I spoke were afraid that they would be sick before they got home, often on the bus, or maybe in a friend's car. The obvious answer would have been to have domiciliary chemotherapy but I had to admit that at that time this was impossible, as specialist nurses were not even thought of at that time. All patients saw a consultant when undergoing chemotherapy. However, things have advanced and chemotherapy is now given nearer people's homes and some cancer centres, such as the Christie Hospital in Manchester, have a mobile unit which travels and parks for the day in populated areas.

Not all the consultants were obstructive to what I was trying to achieve and the cardiologist agreed to let patients have their own notes and X-rays. This worked well and none were lost or mislaid. Patients wanted this, but we have always undermined their ability to be reliable in such matters. I recently read in a letter from a doctor who had undertaken an audit in his paediatric clinic that the medical records were missing in one third of consultations. In another third, the medical records were incomplete with previous letters and summaries missing. When will we learn to trust people?

When general management was introduced, groups of general managers got together to share experiences and learn from each other in their new roles. Because of the work I had done on consumer affairs, I was invited to give presentations to senior staff at the King's Fund in London. I enjoyed sharing with others my findings on what patients really needed and how I had managed, with difficulty, to change things. During these sessions, I became aware of how the Griffiths Report had debased the nursing profession.

Although there were many senior nurses in the audience, not many of them had 'nurse' in their title. Instead, they had changed titles to 'director of quality' or 'director of clinical practice'. I was sad at this outcome and wondered how the public would be able to negotiate their way if they had a matter of concern and they wanted to speak to the most senior nurse. In the old days they would have asked for the matron, but those days had gone.

At that time Brighton Health Authority (BHA) had set up an exchange programme with the George Washington Hospital in Washington USA and I was invited there in 1985. At that time the insurance companies there had challenged the hospitals on the costs of treatments as premiums were rising at a rapid rate. The insurance companies clamped down on how much they would pay for each treatment with the result that the competition between hospitals became widespread. Marketing became important and when I visited the George Washington I was dumbfounded to find that wards were being closed because the new arrangements meant shorter stays and the same number of beds was not required. More and more patients were being treated as outpatients, and this type of care has progressed over the years in all countries.

When I look back to the time when I was a student nurse, patients needing surgery for varicose veins and hernias were kept in for ten days while a cataract extraction required six weeks of bed rest. Now all can be done as day surgery cases.

An exchange that I set up was an exchange of nurses with a university in the States. With the help of my deputy we arranged an interesting programme for them to see our services. We also had a social programme with trips to London and the Theatre Royal in Brighton. In London we lost one student on the Underground, resulting in me walking around for the rest of the time with my umbrella held up in the air just like a tourist guide. Leslie and I entertained them at home and I held a farewell party for them in my office. Happy days.

I was still in charge of the School of Nursing. The members of staff were very apprehensive about their future because of the report on the future of nurse education called Project 2000, as it was to be implemented in all areas by that date. One of the important recommendations was that Schools of Nursing should move into universities with student nurses becoming 'proper' students. With all the advancements in medical procedures, it was no longer feasible to continue with the apprentice type training. This was long overdue.

The school in Brighton operated as an isolated unit, not situated in any hospital nor wishing to come within anyone's control. When I visited it, it was like trying to get into Fort Knox and the staff were uncooperative, to say the least. We had the training of student nurses withdrawn for a year by the examining body, the English National Board. I was very upset and set up an inquiry into the running of the school, as a result of which the training was re-instated. Eventually the school joined up with those of Eastbourne, Hastings and Tunbridge Wells and moved en masse into Brighton University, in line with Project 2000.

The staff at the Brighton School obviously resented me, but the students did not and let me have their research projects to read, two of which I remember well. One was entitled 'Paper on my head does not make me a Nurse'. This student had canvassed her colleagues regarding the wearing of caps that were paper, not the nice fabric of the old days. They did not want to wear them any more. At the time, as always, we were overspent and were seeking ways of saving money. I estimated that £2K per year could be saved on caps and this was accepted as a cost improvement, but to this day I deeply regret it, as caps were the one distinguishing aspect of uniform that other disciplines did not have. The headline in the *Evening Argus* the next day was 'Nurses to lose their caps' with no mention of our overspend.

Another student entitled her study 'Half of Brighton has seen my knickers'. This brought about the wearing of trouser suits, which proved to give better freedom of movement and helped to prevent back injuries, as well as giving a degree of modesty.

One of the big new initiatives to save money was the contracting out of services such as cleaning, laundry and catering. The ward sister lost control of patient nutrition as meals were now served without nursing supervision. The staff of the outside cleaning company were allocated to wards and departments on a daily basis. Therefore these staff were no longer part of the ward team who took great pride in their area of work. Hospital laundries closed and wards became short of bed linen and other essentials.

Some years later, I visited a London teaching hospital and was appalled to read the notices that were everywhere advising patients and relatives that if they wanted to complain about any of the ancillary services they should ring various telephone numbers that were displayed on the notices. The ward sister had lost all control of these vital aspects of the care of the patient, I am pleased to say that there has been a u-turn on the arrangements for those services: the ward sister has regained control of the patients' food and the ward orderly has returned as a team member. In the meantime, of course, we have had the increase in serious infections some of which, such as MRSA, have resulted in deaths.

Since that time we have had many more re-organisations. On the acute side were Foundation Trusts, now NHS Trusts, which have greater autonomy. But that can be questioned while the political football game goes on. On the primary and community care side we have had General Practitioner Fund Holders based on practices, then this changed to Community Care Trusts and now we have Commissioner Groups of GPs, who hold most of the budget for health care and are responsible for purchasing what care is needed from the acute Trusts.

All of these re-organisations have cost vast sums of money as well as loss of expertise from all areas. Gone are the days when chairmen and non-executives held their posts without remuneration except for expenses. They knew their populations, were public spirited and wanted to give something back. Now Trust chairmen earn up to £50,000 and non-executives about £15,000, all of which comes out of the health service budget. Now public-spirited people give up their time for nothing to give the patient/carer/consumer input, so that services are user-friendly. Whether their voice is listened to is open to debate.

It is regrettable that with all the changes, the legacy of the Griffiths Report remains with us as far as nursing and nurses are concerned. This ensures that, in most places, nursing has not returned to its rightful position as professionals responsible for 24/7 care of patients, but operates with its hands tied behind its back. The director of nursing on the Trust board, a position that had to be fought for to get it in statute, has to make the case for better patient care against the backdrop of the Trust having to make savings often referred to as 'cost improvement programmes'. Whether there is any improvement in the care of patients is also open to debate.

We have seen an increase in general managers, deputy general managers and assistant general managers at unit and divisional levels. This is not surprising, especially since the setting of targets. At divisional level there is a matron responsible for the standard of care and the budget, but a large part of the matron's time is spent arguing with the general managers whose main responsibilities appear to be meeting targets and saving money. Yet the matron is the one who is responsible for achieving the targets and at the same time ensuring safe care. A recent Care Quality Commission report has identified this as a major problem in advancing good practice.

As 'chief nursing advisor' I was expected to advise on nursing matters, but that advice was not always welcome and at times not sought. One such occasion was regarding mental health services. At that time the large psychiatric hospitals that contained patients from an extensive geographical area were closing. Patients were to be relocated back to their area of former residency so as to be near relatives. St. Francis Hospital at Haywards Heath was therefore discharging patients back to smaller more friendly units in Brighton. BHA was negotiating costs and identifying suitable venues to house the patients. The general manager for psychiatric services produced a paper for the board meeting, the contents of which I had not even seen let alone discussed with her.

At the meeting I innocently asked what the percentage of mentally qualified nurses, i.e. registered mental nurses (RMN), would be in each unit. To my consternation the answer was that there would not be any RMNs in the units, only carers who would have three weeks' training. This was a public meeting and yet I had to challenge this arrangement. Following discussion I was supported by the Authority members who took my point that qualified nurses would be required in each unit. Unfortunately, this was not the only time I had to step in to avoid unsafe care. It was an example of how little some general managers appreciated safe patient care.

In 1990 I had been in Brighton for six years and thought it was time to move on. One of the reasons was that the chairman, Julia Cumberlege, was leaving her position and I knew that things would not be the same. I had the utmost respect for her and I knew that she had appreciated my input to the Authority. During her time in Brighton, at the request of the Government of the day, she had produced the report on Community Nursing and also a report on Midwifery Services. This meant that she was often away from home and she joked that her three sons, all in their early teens, threatened to ask to be taken into care. On one occasion when I was going to meet her at her home to brief her on a paper that was going to the board meeting, I rang her home to see when would be a convenient time. Her son answered the phone and informed me in a pained voice that he had no idea when she would be home, but that he had to put the chops in the oven at a certain time.

Julia became Baroness Cumberlege not long after and I was delighted when she became speaker on health services in the House of Lords. She later put together a programme called 'The Westminster Experience' for senior health service personnel. This involves acquiring an increased knowledge of how political thinking is translated into policy and implemented, as well as an increased awareness on how to influence the political agenda on a national and regional level. It helped staff to navigate through the political minefield. I wish I had undertaken the programme before moving on to my next post as regional nursing officer for the North Thames Regional Health Authority.

My time in Brighton had been challenging and frustrating. It had been satisfying in that I learn a lot about patients' needs and felt I had contributed to better care on the whole. It was also a socially enjoyable time and that was mainly because of the people I was working with, especially the general manager, David Bowden, the chief medical officer Glenwin Williams who was an eccentric Welshman, and the treasurer, Jim Henry, an astute Scotsman. David's wife, Pauline, always looked after Leslie at official functions when David and I were involved with looking after VIPs.

We remained friends after we left the area and had many dinner parties in each others' homes. We and the Bowdens were great cricket enthusiasts and we spent many happy days watching test matches and one-day internationals as well as county cricket. I remember one day at Lord's when a young man, the worst for wear, was shouting abuse at the players and we were all getting annoyed. This was not cricket. Pauline tapped him on the shoulder and said in a loud voice 'Were you born a complete idiot or have you been working at it for years?' The abusive comments stopped as the people around us fell about laughing

All during my career I have had a friend and mentor, Audrey Emerton. We had both worked in the South Thames Region and had come across each other at various times. Audrey wrote me a letter of congratulations when I became national chairman of the NATN. She advised me to apply for a regional nursing officer post. At that time the vacancy was in the North East Thames Regional Health Authority. This would be a more strategic role that involved planning for the future. It would not enable me to have the patient contact that I enjoyed, but one of the attractions was that I would be responsible for all non-medical education.

Although not an academic, I had been a member of the English National Board, the organisation for the inspection and approval for all nursing courses, from 1983 to 1988. In 1985, we produced a strategy that has been described as concepts rather than recommendations on the future of nurse education. This outlined training based on an initial 18 months to become a practical nurse and a further 18 months to become a registered nurse. I had also been a member of the National Training Authority from 1988 to 1991. It was the United Kingdom Central Council who eventually produced Project 2000 that was implemented, but I still think the English National Board strategy had much to recommend it. Now we have so many care assistants who are not registered in any way.

Care assistants can be dismissed from a job for abuse of patients and still get another job quite easily, because of a lack of commitment by successive governments to introduce registration for this grade of staff. The Francis Report also recommended registration following the appalling care at mid-Staffordshire, but again the Government has refused to take this necessary action. What needs to happen before action will be taken?

In hindsight, maybe at this stage I should have applied for a general manager post, but I was aware that very few nurses were successful when applying. I remember only one, Christine Hancock, who became a general manager and later became general secretary of the Royal College of Nursing. It was obvious that senior nurses were being marginalised and were not seen as leaders and managers. Rather, the perception still remained that we were the handmaidens of the medical profession and were treated as such. Doctors were encouraged to apply for these posts as it was hoped that they would make their colleagues toe the line when it came to implementing the policies of the government of the day.

REGIONAL NURSING OFFICER

So I became regional nursing officer for North East Thames in 1990 and left in 1993, or should I say kicked out in that year? For a time I enjoyed my new role. It involved giving advice to nurses and ensuring that they were supported. I had monthly meetings with the chief nurse advisors in the districts, some of whom had lost the 'nurse' from their titles, as had others at unit level. There was no longer any kudos in having 'nurse' in your title, rather the reverse in the eyes of general managers who appeared to be out to settle old scores.

I enjoyed my role as lead director for education and training and introduced the recommendations in line with Project 2000. Schools of Nursing were amalgamated and then integrated into universities. With the help of the chief executive of the English National Board, Tony Smith, we were the first to integrate the schools of Nursing in Essex into what was then the Anglia Polytechnic University and is now Anglia Ruskin University. This was achieved following many hours of negotiation as it included transferring budgets. Tony was a 'can do' person and without him I do not know if I would have been successful.

I accepted an invitation to present the certificates to the students for the University at Chelmsford Cathedral and it was a wonderful day. I presented at other graduation ceremonies around the Region and I really enjoyed talking to the newly qualified students.

The amalgamation of schools was not done without a great deal of negotiation, some of which became very heated. One especially difficult one involved the Bloomsbury School of Nurse Education and City University. The school head at Bloomsbury was adamant that 'her' school should remain as it was and we had the most animated discussions with her storming out of my office and banging the door. It was just before Christmas and I decided to leave matters alone until after the holiday. Leslie and I went to the Canaries for a break. We were in a supermarket one day and I whispered to Leslie not to move but to concentrate on the shelf in front of us. The poor man did not know what was happening, but I had spied the school head just near us and the last thing I wanted, while on holiday, was to have another heated argument.

I became involved in the Junior Doctors' Steering Group as we were introducing the European Directorate on junior doctors' hours which required them not to work longer than a set number of hours. We were looking at the roles of nurses and how they could include duties which were previously the province of junior doctors. There was tremendous political pressure to reduce junior doctors' hours, and whereas I was supportive of nurses reaching their full potential, I was aware that for this to happen successfully, it needed careful planning of manpower, education and training. There was the opportunity for nurses to grab status and money by taking on duties and functions previously done by medical staff, but not at the expense of neglecting good nursing care. I felt that nurses needed to proceed with caution or they might lose the respect of the public and their credibility as professionals.

An amusing episode, at my expense, happened at about this time. Some senior staff from Northern Ireland were shadowing me as they were interested in the work I was doing. At the end of their time, they asked if they could come back and could it be at the same time as U2? I had not a clue as to what they were talking about and told them that I did not know if we were having new computers. They just could not believe that I did not know who U2 were. I was Irish and U2 were top of the charts.

At the end of 1992, everything changed. A new general manager was appointed and it was obvious from the beginning that my face did not fit. Nothing I did was appreciated, it appeared that decisions were being made without any discussion with me and my involvement was not required. When I returned from the Christmas break, rumours abounded that I would be leaving before long. I was devastated and became very stressed. It was an unhappy time for many as the Regions were amalgamating, yet another reorganisation that I would need to live through. The Regions were being reduced from fifteen to eight and North East and North West Thames were to become one.

The vice-chairman, Baroness Gardner, came to see me as she had heard the rumours and was adamant that she would not allow me to go. At that stage, I knew that there was no going back. I could not work with the general manager who had told me that he wanted me to leave. I negotiated early retirement and left just before Easter, as I had a holiday booked, and then did not return. I was too upset to even tell my small staff, who were allocated to various departments after I left. The Regional Nursing Department was no more. Looking back, I think the final nail in my coffin was when I refused point blank to lose 'nurse' from my title. The other reason I had to go was because I had the budget for all non-medical education. The general manager wanted it to go to the personnel director to manage and with it would go an increase in salary as this would be based on how much finance one controlled. This happened after I left.

The atmosphere at that time was one of mistrust and nastiness. Macho management was the order of the day and it is interesting when I look back to reflect that it was female nurses at all levels who were treated badly. The senior male nurses were not challenged in their positions. Ten years after the Griffiths Report, nurses continued to be marginalised as nurses are mostly female, while doctors, mostly male, were considered to have their uses and were not treated the same. On this front there has been little change for women in all walks of life.

When my departure became common knowledge I had letters from many of the chairmen in the Region who felt that my departure from the NHS was a loss. I appreciated these messages as I was very sad at how my career had ended. Lunch and dinner parties were arranged around the Region and these gave me the opportunity to thank people for their support and to say goodbye properly. I knew I had to move on. The health service was still in my blood so I started as a consultant on many health-linked projects. I was asked to be on panels involving medical accidents, one of which was in Scotland. The chief nursing officer wanted a nurse not connected with Scotland. A young mother had died following a mistake with the administration of pain relieving drugs. I was amazed to find that the Health Authority non-executive member, a barrister who chaired the panel of inquiry, thought that the director of nursing in the hospital had authority over all nursing staff when this was now the responsibility of the general managers at unit level. The nurses had not been trained in the administration of the drugs and the death had occurred through ignorance. The coroner had criticised the hospital for being neglectful.

I undertook audits in nursing and residential care homes investigating standards of care and the documentation of the care delivered. I investigated a religious organisation and the running of its infirmary where the elderly nuns were being cared for. I undertook a survey of operating theatres and recommended how improvements could be made. I acted as facilitator in the production of a risk assessment guide for operating theatres.

Since my days as a member of the panel on the Shewan Inquiry, I have remained interested in the law. I was approached to give an expert opinion on litigation involving medical accidents, especially where operating theatres were involved. This on one or two occasions meant appearing in court, a very challenging experience.

During my career, I wrote and had published many articles on nursing and health service matters. I continued with this work and was delighted to be appointed an Arena Columnist for the *Nursing Times* during 1995. I have always enjoyed writing and this is one of the reasons that I have written this book.

EAST BERKSHIRE COMMUNITY TRUST

I was approached, and applied to become a non-executive on a community care trust in the area and when the chairman of the trust retired I was appointed chairman. This was in 1998 and I was not long into the post when yet another re-organisation was underway. The community care trust was to be broken up into three primary care group (PCGs) and it was my role to lead this change without too much disruption to services.

The executives in the Trust were possibly suffering from re-organisational fatigue and most planned to take early retirement if possible. Eyes were taken off the ball and my first shock was to receive a letter from the Royal College of Ophthalmologists to say that our training of junior doctors was to be withdrawn. It was alleged that the Trust had not fulfilled their recommendation at the last inspection to appoint a fourth consultant. I called an emergency meeting and asked the executives why the report had not come to the board. As a non-executive I had not seen it. There was silence as they knew they were in the wrong. I then met the three consultants in the Eye Unit at the King Edward VII Hospital and asked them if they were aware that a fourth consultant had to be appointed. They knew about the report but informed me that they did not want a fourth consultant. When asked why they replied that it would interfere with their private practice, i.e. the private work would have to be shared between four and not three. An advertisement was placed and a fourth consultant was appointed.

As well as the King Edward VII Hospital, there were two other small community hospitals in the Trust. The acute trust for the area had cut staff numbers and these were mostly qualified nurses. The chief executive for the community trust and I were called to a meeting with our opposite numbers in the acute trust and 'ordered' to cut our numbers of qualified nurses in line with the acute trust. I was aware that the community had adequate numbers and that to cut staff would affect patient care. I refused point blank to do so. This was not welcome and no doubt was reported up the line to those responsible for making non-executive appointments.

One of the highlights, if not the only one, of my chairmanship was when the Queen came to open the refurbished eye hospital, the King Edward VII Hospital at Windsor. I had been advised that one must always ask the Queen if one wanted royalty to be involved in Windsor. The Queen accepted our invitation and the event was arranged for 9th November 2000. There were many meetings to organise the visit and eventually an interesting programme was put together involving the eye unit where new equipment had been installed, the audiology unit where new soundproof units had been installed and a tour of the refurbished facilities for outpatients. I was advised that as we were presenting a bouquet to her Majesty we should ensure that there was no wire in it, as wire ruins the gloves. The great day came. I was a bag of nerves, but managed to show her Majesty around as arranged and she was interested in everything.

We had a small reception in the board room afterwards, at which the Queen met various staff who had been involved in the refurbishing and also the chairman of the League of Friends, Colleen Jones, who had been so helpful in last minute supply of such things as pictures for the walls.

At that time there was a big push to reduce waiting lists. The one I was involved with was the waiting list for eye surgery. The aim was that all operations should be done with no one waiting more than three months. Extra money was made available for the consultants to do extra operating sessions at weekends. They were the same consultants, so what was the incentive for them to lengthen their normal lists when extra money was available to them for the extra sessions?

On one occasion, we overshot the three months because of a recording error and I was hauled in front of the regional chairman, a business man and financier, who tore me off a strip, was very rude and informed me that as the community trust was to be no more, I should not bother to apply for any other vacancy. The chair of the acute trust was to be advertised in the next few months. He also informed me that he had no intention of 'stuffing' the new PCGs with members of the community trust when it would be disbanded. New blood from outside the health service was what was required. To me, this was the precursor of the bullying that is now common in the health service and is so destructive to morale. It is no wonder this bullying takes place when one watches Question Time in the House of Commons.

During my chairmanship of the Community Trust, I became more aware of the lack of coordination between acute services, community services and social services. Northern Ireland had amalgamated community services and social services during the nineties and I sent two members of staff there to find out how it was working.

Ann Hughes, an occupational therapist and Penny Asquith, a physiotherapist, reported that there was not a great deal of cooperation between the two organisations except where both were in the same building. Community staff and social service staff were both vying for position and the tribal warfare continued. Successive governments in Britain have promised to amalgamate them, but I doubt if it will ever happen as health care is free at the point of delivery while social services are means-tested. It will be a suicidal government that will do away with free at the point of delivery for health services and in the present economic situation social services will continue to be means-tested. Will this prevent better integration that has been talked about for years with little action?

The remainder of my chairmanship was taken up overseeing the reorganisation (another one) into three PCGs, who were to transfer powers to GPs. Later they became primary care trusts (PCTs). We had many meetings with the three groups, at one of which we were referred to as the living dead. I was concerned for the staff who were not sure for whom they would be working in the future, who would pay their salaries and to whom they would be responsible. I held many meetings with them, trying to reassure them that there would still be patients to look after and so they would remain employees, even if I could not spell out which organisation they would be working for.

One of the results of this reorganisation was that all notepaper had to be changed and hours were spent rewriting procedures for each of the three Groups. It may seem petty to complain about notepaper being thrown out, but if you multiplied this cost across the whole of the country, it would come to a tidy sum, money that could be better spent. But with every change of government, it would seem that we must reorganise the health service with no regard for the cost or the anxieties of staff and patients.

Some staff hoped that I would apply for the chairmanship of Windsor and Maidenhead PCG, where I lived. My own GP was one of the prominent doctors on that group. The area chairman asked to meet me for coffee at a posh hotel and informed me that I should not apply as the other GPs in the group might resent the fact that I had known my GP for a long time. I was too dumbfounded to say anything and it was only later that I woke up to the fact that my integrity was being challenged.

The irony of it all was that I had no intention of applying for any more posts. I had seen what was happening to the health service. It appeared to me that business people and financiers were the future managers. I also thought that 'yes' people were required to do the bidding of the politicians. I did not have the reputation of being a 'yes' person.

THE FLORENCE NIGHTINGALE FOUNDATION

I had lost faith in the management of the health service but I never lost faith in my own profession of nursing. This was confirmed when I took over as director of the Florence Nightingale Foundation in 1996. I had been approached by the then director, Hope Trenchard. Hope had been a colleague at regional level but had retired before me. She was not a well person and we had arranged to meet in September, but she died before we met so I had no handover from her. The chairman, Mo Acland, contacted me and we met. I agreed to become the director and it was the best move I have ever made. I spent almost fourteen years in the post before I finally retired in 2010, during which I met some amazingly inspirational nurses and midwives at all levels.

The Statement of Purpose of the Foundation reads as follows: 'The Florence Nightingale Foundation – a living memorial to Florence Nightingale – advances the study of nursing and promotes excellence in nursing practice. The Foundation raises funds to provide scholarships for nurses, midwives and health visitors to study at home and abroad, to promote innovation in practice, to extend knowledge and skills to meet changing needs. The Foundation promotes the special contribution of nursing to society and to the health of people. It encourages international understanding and learning between nurses.'

At the time the Florence Nightingale Foundation was located in a basement office in the Red Cross headquarters in Grosvenor Crescent. Leslie used to refer to it as my 'Dickensian den'. The desks were old with drawers that did not open. We had an old typewriter with jammed keys and most writing was done in longhand. The reports of scholars of the Foundation that should have gone to the Royal College of Nursing Library were still in the office. It was obvious that with Hope having been ill there was a great deal of catching up to do.

Joanna Sterry had been the secretary for 26 years and, although a great help to me as a beginner, was looking to retire and did so nine months after I started. Ann Fisher, who had worked in the diplomatic corps, replaced her and remained with the Foundation until 2000. Ann put in some good office practices that were long overdue but was resistant to up-to-date technology, such as going on the internet and developing a website. We would have to embrace new technology if we were going to bring the Foundation up-to-date. In 2001, Pamela Mummery joined as administrator and company secretary.

She was very experienced, having been a librarian and then working at a senior level for the Metropolitan Police. She is Irish by background, has a great sense of humour and we hit it off from the beginning. I was fortunate to have her with me until I retired and we remain very good friends.

The awarding of scholarships was our principal function and I set out to raise funds so that we could increase the number of nurses we could help to improve practice. In my first year we awarded fifteen scholarships for travel, twelve for research and we also awarded funds to eleven enrolled nurses to undertake further training to become registered nurses.

The travel scholarships allowed nurses to travel in Britain or abroad to visit other units in their speciality and access centres of excellence. The research helped nurses investigate ways to improve care so that it became evidence-based and not 'do as I do', as happened in my days as a junior nurse. The sponsors and the Foundation were adamant that all scholarships should have outcomes to improve care. We tried hard to prevent costly studies that did not alter practice but produced reports that ended up gathering dust on library shelves. When interviewing candidates, they were often asked what piece of research they had implemented in their practice recently.

Even today I remain concerned that the amount of money being invested in nursing research is not always bearing fruit for the benefit of patients, but then I admit that I am not a researcher. My investigation into theatre staffing all those years ago would probably not be classed as research today because of the advancement in methodology.

The Foundation awarded fellowships to nurses who had undertaken a scholarship and then progressed in their career. The fellows were instrumental in encouraging others to apply and often mentored new scholars. My colleague, Tony Smith, became a fellow and came on to the executive of the Foundation and contributed greatly to the advancement of the organisation. As I mentioned earlier, Tony was a 'can do' person and if I was concerned about something Tony would come out with 'Now, just WHAT is the problem? We got the blankets out of the barracks in Scutari, we cut through the red tape, of course we can handle it'. Tony's untimely death in 2004 was a sad loss to the profession and I missed him greatly as a colleague and friend.

I had not long been with the Foundation when I realised that we had done a poor job in public relations by not ensuring that everyone knew of the changes in our profession. The Goldsmiths' Livery Company gave the Foundation a travel scholarship each year. In my second year I received a telephone call from their clerk telling me that I had made a mistake and had awarded their scholarship to a non-nurse. I was surprised at this as we checked all applicants with the registering body to ensure that they were bona fide nurses. I asked why he thought that the scholar was not a nurse and the reply was that it was a man. The clerk informed me that their awarding committee was unaware that we had male nurses.

The highlight each year was the Florence Nightingale Commemoration Service at Westminster Abbey. It needed a great deal of organisation, but was always worth the effort as it is a beautiful service at which the profession rededicates its commitment to the care of patients. Early each year a meeting is held with the Dean of the Abbey and his staff to confirm the date, which is always close to Florence Nightingale's birthday on 12th May. Music, hymns, the readings and the readers, the intercessions and, most importantly, who is giving the address, are all agreed at this meeting.

At the Service the Florence Nightingale lamp, which is kept in the Nurses' Chapel (now the Florence Nightingale Chapel), is carried in procession by one of our scholars and is escorted by student nurses from one of the universities. The lamp is passed between nurses of different grades and branches of nursing on the steps of the sacrarium and it is then passed to the Dean who places it on the altar. This represents the transmission of knowledge from one nurse to another and highlights the diversity of care given by nurses for the benefit of humanity. The Nurses' Roll of Honour, containing the names of nurses killed in the Second World War, is carried by a junior member of the armed forces and is escorted in procession by the three Matrons-in-Chief of Her Majesty's Armed Forces. The Abbey is silent apart from the footsteps of those in the procession and it is a very moving time during the service.

When I started at the Foundation, the Abbey was not always full, so letters were sent to all hospitals and colleges of nursing as well as getting publicity for the service in the media. At my last service in 2010 the Abbey was not just full, but extra seating had to be installed – that may have had something to do with Archbishop Tutu giving the address. However, in the years in between, the Abbey was full.

Other Florence Nightingale services are also held in May and one of the most inspiring is in St Margaret's Church in East Wellow in Hampshire where Florence Nightingale is buried. It is a very old Norman church and after the simple service prayers are read at the graveside. A service is held in Northern Ireland most years and I have had the honour of reading a lesson one year as well as attending in other years. I formed close ties with the Florence Nightingale Committee there and through them met Mona Grey who became a friend. Mona was most helpful in encouraging me to get a higher profile for the Foundation. She had worked as night superintendent at the London Hospital during the Blitz and would tell scary stories of running across London Bridge from the nurses' home to the hospital with bombs falling. She also told of the evacuation of wards when the hospital was hit. It was through a legacy from Mona that recently the RCN Publishing Company produced a book entitled 'Nurses' Voices' that relates the experiences of nurses during the Troubles in Northern Ireland. It contained a lot of frightening stories which Mona would have identified with. She became first the general secretary of the RCN in Northern Ireland and then the chief nursing officer in Northern Ireland. She was a formidable lady and whatever Mona decreed had to happen.

In 1999, Mona asked me to give the second History of Nursing Lecture at the University of Ulster. This was a challenge, I am not an historian, an academic or a researcher, but 'she who must be obeyed' would have none of my excuses. I decided that I would link nursing at that time with the teachings of Florence Nightingale which are still pertinent. I called my lecture 'Florence Nightingale – a legacy for today'.

I stressed that she was visible as she walked through the four miles of beds in the barrack hospital in Scutari, comforting the injured and dying soldiers and supporting the staff, not like some of the directors of nursing today who never visit their hospital wards. She was tenacious in ensuring that supplies of food and blankets were released from the quartermaster's store and she upset people in the process. She had a vision for the future of nursing and the Army and ensured that a Royal Commission into the running of the Army was set up after the disasters that she witnessed during the Crimean War. Her tenacity ensured that she had an audience with Queen Victoria to bring this about and I questioned our tenacity today in ensuring safe levels of care.

At one stage Florence Nightingale wrote that in nursing while the intellectual foot has made a step in advance, the practical foot has remained behind. She would have been appalled at the number of research reports gathering dust on library shelves. She was knowledgeable, well-educated and became a founder member of the Statistical Society at Oxford University. She would have welcomed the reforms in nurse education but would have expected better-educated nurses to give better patient care.

She also wrote 'It may seem a strange principle to enunciate, as a first requirement in a hospital, that it should do the sick no harm'. She would be turning in her grave at the recent revelations that have been reported on some of our hospitals today. There has been a great rise in hospital infections as a result of the misuse and overuse of antibiotics. In her day there were no antibiotics and hygiene was essential. We have all seen the devastating results from outbreaks of MRSA and *C. difficile* and the blame has been firmly placed on lack of hygiene, poor nursing practice and poor leadership and management by boards of Trusts.

After the lecture Mona presented me with an inscribed glass bowl and I think of her whenever I use it. She is another friend that I miss following her death in 2009, just before her hundredth birthday.

The year 1999 was a special year because of other events as well. It was the centenary of the International Council of Nurses, and a celebration was held in London and hosted by the Royal College of Nursing. The Foundation, in association with the Royal College of Nursing and the International Council of Nurses took part in a service at Westminster Abbey in July. It was a multi-faith service and I was given the honour of reading a lesson. As a friend pointed out to me, I was the only Catholic to read from the Koran in an Anglican Abbey.

Over the years, I became aware that student nurses knew very little about Florence Nightingale and the history of nursing. In 1999, a students' day was held for the first time, and has continued every year, with up to seventy attending, on the same day as the Abbey Service. In the morning, the students put questions to a panel of senior nurses, and lively discussion follows. After lunch they visit the Florence Nightingale Museum at St Thomas' Hospital and in the evening they attend the service. I was surprised at how popular the day became and I received many letters from the attendees saying how much they appreciated the day, how much they had learned and how the day had opened their eyes to their rich heritage.

The number of scholarships that we could award each year depended on the funds received from our sponsors and every endeavour was made to increase the funds. Our sponsors came from a range of organisations. I have already mentioned the Goldsmiths' Company, but they were not the only livery company to provide money. We were lucky to have as a trustee a representative of the Lord Mayor's office who was a great help in securing funds. Over the years, we received funds from the Mercers', Drapers', Salters' and Girdlers' Companies.

The Band Trust (the B and D referred to Barbara and David Karmel) was managed by the Honourable Mr and Mrs Wallop. Lavinia Wallop is the Karmels' daughter. The Band Trust has been extremely generous to the Foundation over the years, providing funds for research and travel. Lavinia helped out with the selection of research scholars and gave the public view on what was required. She became a friend as did Michael Macfadyen who supervised the Sandra Trust. Sandra was the dog of a rich businessman and when the dog died this gentleman left a legacy to enable nurses to travel and study abroad. Eventually the four health departments of the UK came on board and provided scholarships for nurses in their country. There were many others to whom the Foundation owed a great deal of gratitude and without whom we could not function.

The Burdett Trust was another from whom we greatly benefited. The Burdett Trust for Nursing is an independent charitable trust named after Sir Henry Burdett, the founder of the Royal National Pension Fund for Nurses. The Trust was set up in recognition of the foundation, philosophy and structure of the Royal National Pension Fund for Nurses.

When it was set up in 2003 we applied for funding and were awarded funds for our research that allowed us to award twenty research scholarships. The Burdett Trust also awarded funds that allowed us to award three leadership scholarships to senior nurses in 2004. Back in 1998 we had hosted a symposium on the leadership challenge facing nursing. Baroness Jay, who gave the keynote address, advised the invited audience that Florence Nightingale was a leader who was not to be defeated by the scale of the task nor by the fear of rocking the boat. She advised nurses to do the same.

One of our scholars who spoke explained that now that general managers controlled nursing budgets and questioned nursing roles, nurse leaders had been given enormous tasks. They were to create environments and provide leadership resulting in quality services at a time when their own roles within the organisational structure were in question. The Griffiths Report lives on.

It was evident that there were limited opportunities for senior nurses to gain an understanding of the potential for their leadership role in the changing world of health care. The three leadership scholarships awarded to senior nurses in 2004 gave them the opportunity to pursue bespoke leadership programmes which would enable them to reach the top positions in nursing. They would be able to prove that they had the necessary skills to lead the profession.

The following year BUPA also provided funds to increase the number of leadership scholarships and we awarded six. In 2009, the year I decided to call it a day, I was delighted to be asked to apply and was successful in becoming a Burdett partner after a strenuous interview before a selection panel. This partnership meant that the Foundation was awarded a sum of £250,000 for three years to support the leadership initiative. I thought that an award to help develop the leadership role was needed, so I was delighted.

Over the years the finances of the Foundation fluctuated in line with the stock market, affecting available resources to run the organisation, but we were fortunate in having organisations that stepped in to fill the gap. The Girdlers agreed to fund the students' day. BUPA agreed to fund the service in the Abbey. When our computer needed upgrading, the Girdlers helped with the cost.

The presentation of certificates is the occasion when the outcome of all our scholarships is shared with our sponsors, supporters and other influential organisations and people. This is now held in the Girdlers' Hall, a beautiful building in the City. At the award ceremony the scholars give an account of the benefits that their scholarships have made to their practice and the delivery of care to patients and clients. All express their appreciation of the sponsors and share with the audience how the experience has developed their skills as practitioners. The feedback we receive is that the changes made were inspirational.

Two scholars who stand out in my memory are Comfort Momo and Lyn Phair. Comfort went to many African countries to investigate female genital mutilation (FGM) and is now an authority on this topical, important subject. She has been interviewed by the media and runs a clinic at St. Thomas' Hospital for those who have undergone this barbaric practice.

Lyn Phair's scholarship took her to Australia to investigate services and facilities for elderly people. Her report was interesting and pointed out how things need to change in this country. She is now a consultant advising on services for the elderly. She has been on our television screens commenting on the recently revealed abuse in our care homes.

I gave notice to the Foundation that I would leave following the commemoration service in May 2010. It not only turned out to be a special occasion, but the whole of 2010 became a very special year for me. In April I received a letter informing me that I was to be awarded Commander of the British Empire (CBE) for my services to nursing and healthcare. I was extremely surprised and felt very honoured. I could not tell anyone (although I did tell Leslie) and it was very difficult for me to keep it to myself until it was announced in the Queen's Birthday Honours list in June.

The commemoration service at the Abbey was a huge success and it was a nightmare trying to fit everyone in. Requests for tickets outnumbered capacity even though the Abbey staff agreed to extra seating. I was approached by a minor canon who wanted me to take part in the intercessions and I was very proud to do it. For me, the evening was very emotional and during the reception after the service the Dean gave a little speech on my achievements. Following discussions with the Dean earlier in the year, he agreed that the Nurses' Chapel should be named the Florence Nightingale Chapel to mark the centenary of Florence Nightingale's death. Another honour for me was reading a poem at Florence's graveside in East Wellow.

In this extraordinary year I was invited to give the after dinner vote of thanks to the Girdlers' Company. I knew that the audience would be totally male, made up of gentlemen of the City, and I felt very apprehensive about the whole thing. But the members of the Girdlers had become friends and had been so generous over the years that I felt I could not refuse. I was warned by our representative from the Lord Mayor's office that 'sex and the City' do not mix. At the same time I needed to add a bit of humour to the address. I also knew that they would expect me to tell Irish jokes and this is one of the best that I shared with them. The Girdlers had recently had their Hall extended so I told the joke about the Irish labourer, Paddy, on top of a building. Two foremen were watching from below when suddenly Paddy took off and landed on the ground, fatally injured. One foreman looked at the other and asked what made him do that. The other foreman, scratching his head replied that before Paddy went to the top of the building, he had asked him what he did in the War and the foreman had told him that he used to fly in Wellingtons.

Early in the year I had approached the BBC to dedicate 'Songs of Praise' to Florence Nightingale because it was the centenary of her death. They agreed, and the programme was shown in July. In it, nurses were interviewed, the presenter had gone to Istanbul and filmed the Barrack Hospital, I was interviewed about Florence Nightingale in her chapel, and there were shots of me 'marshalling the troops' during the rehearsals before the service. I was delighted with the programme as it raised the profile of the Foundation.

The climax of the year, of course, was my investiture at Windsor Castle by the Queen in November. My family came over from Ireland and none of us will forget the day. Following the investiture we had lunch and in the evening my dear friend, Audrey, hosted a dinner for us all in the House of Lords. As we drove back home, I reflected not only on the great day, the amazing year and the great honour, but also on the wonderful career I had had, warts and all.

BIBLIOGRAPHY

Association of Perioperative Registered Nurses (1967) Teaching the Operating Room Technician. Association of Operating Room Nurses (AORN), Denver

Briggs Report (1972) The Report of the Committee on Nursing. HMSO, London

Cumberlege Report (1986) Neighbourhood Nursing – a focus for care. The Community Nursing Review. Department of Health and Social Security. HMSO, London

Graham M, Orr J (2013) Nurses' Voices from the Northern Ireland Troubles. RCN Publishing, London

Grey Book (1972) Management Arrangements on the Reorganised Health Service. HMSO, London

Griffiths Inquiry (1983) NHS Management Inquiry Report. DHSS, London

Kensington and Chelsea and Westminster Area Health Authority (Teaching) (1977) Abridged Report [of The] Committee of Inquiry [into the Incident Affecting Miss Elizabeth Shewan.]. Shewan Inquiry. National Archives, Kew, Ref. MH/160/1154 to 1158

Lewin Report (1970) The Organisation and Staffing of Operating Departments. Department of Health and Social Security. HMSO, London

Merrison Commission (1979) Royal Commission on the NHS. HMSO, London

Salmon Report (1966) Report of the Committee on Senior Nursing Staff Structure. HMSO, London

The Mid Staffordshire NHS Foundation Trust Public Inquiry (2013) Report of the Mid Staffordshire NHS Foundation Trust Public Inquiry. Francis Report. The Stationery Office, London

The Westminster Experience (www.cumberlegeeden.co.uk)

United Kingdom Central Council for Nursing, Midwifery, and Health Visiting (1986) Project 2000 A New Preparation for Practice. United Kingdom Central Council for Nursing, Midwifery, and Health Visiting, London

Lectures, presentations and scholarship reports by Mary Donn/Spinks

Donn M (1973) A Report on Research into "The Training and Function Integration of the Nurse and Allied Personnel in the Operating Theatre in Britain" NATNews February

Donn M (1973) A Report on "The Training and Function Integration of the Nurse and Allied Personnel in the Operating Theatre in the USA." NATNews June

Donn M (1978) Theatre Nurses meet Changing Social Needs. AORN Journal September

Donn M (1988) "Educate that you may be Free". Daisy Ayris Lecture. NATNews

Spinks M (1999) Florence Nightingale - a legacy for today. Mona Grey History of Nursing Lecture

Spinks M (1999) Foundations of Nursing: Nightingale's Legacy. International History of Nursing Journal 5(1): Winter

Spinks M (2006) "Looking back, looking forward". Daisy Ayris Lecture. NATNews 6(1)

GLOSSARY

A&E	Accident and Emergency
AfPP	Association for Peri-operative Practice
AGM	Annual General Meeting
ANA	American Nurses Association
AORN	Association of Operating Room Nurses
AORT	Association of Operating Room Technicians
AST	Association of Surgical Technologists
BHA	Brighton Health Authority
CBE	Commander of the British Empire
CNO	Chief Nursing Officer
COPD	College of Operating Department Practice
CSSD	Central Sterile Supply Department
ENB	English National Board
FGM	Female Genital Mutilation
FNF	Florence Nightingale Foundation
FRCS	Fellow of the Royal College of Surgeons
GP	General Practitioner
ICN	International Council of Nurses
ICU	Intensive Care Unit
IOTT	Institute of Theatre Technicians
ITU	Intensive Therapy Unit
MBE	Member of the British Empire
MRSA	Meticillin-resistant *Staphylococcus aureus*
NATN	National Association of Theatre Nurses

NO	Nursing Officer
OBE	Order of the British Empire
ODA	Operating Department Assistant
OPD	Operating Department Practitioner
OR	Operating Room
ORT	Operating Room Technician
PCG	Primary Care Group
PCT	Primary Care Trust
QC	Queen's Council
RAF	Royal Air Force
RCN	Royal College of Nursing
RMN	Registered Mental Nurse
RNO	Regional Nursing Officer
RNPFN	Royal National Pension Fund for Nurses
SNO	Senior Nursing Officer
TSSU	Theatre Sterile Supply Department
UKCC	United Kingdom Central Council